THE IRON FLUTE

THE IRON FLUTE
War Poetry from
Ancient & Medieval China

Selected, translated and introduced by
Kevin Maynard

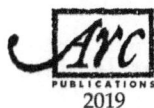

Arc
PUBLICATIONS
2019

Published by Arc Publications,
Nanholme Mill, Shaw Wood Road
Todmorden OL14 6DA, UK
www.arcpublications.co.uk

978 1911469 10 0 (pbk)
978 1911469 11 7 (hbk)

Design by Tony Ward

Cover picture:
Design based on Han dynasty stone rubbing
of a warrior riding to war

LOTTERY FUNDED

Supported using public funding by
ARTS COUNCIL
ENGLAND

**Arc Publications 'Anthologies in Translation'
Series Editor: Jean Boase-Beier**

for
Professor J. P. Seaton
and David Su Liqun
苏立群 / 蘇立群

CONTENTS

Many who have little or no knowledge of Chinese culture will still have heard of Sunzi's *Art of War*[1]. But what of the art inspired by war?[2]

The visual arts in China have nearly always avoided depicting scenes of conflict. Its literature on the other hand often finds warfare an irresistibly alluring topic – and in this respect it is of course no different from most other world literatures, whether oral or written.

While Chinese prose has done ample justice to this theme (one has only to think of novels such as *Outlaws of the Marsh* or *The Three Kingdoms*) it is poetry that can boast the most ancient lineage, since it antedates the first Chinese novels by almost two millennia.

Two sub-genres in particular stand out, only one of which has up to now been well served by translators. The first is called 'border poetry' (its Chinese name is 邊塞詩 biānsài shī); this is sometimes also described as the 'frontier style' (邊塞體 biānsài tǐ). The second is known as 喪亂詩 sāngluàn shī – which we have to translate, rather clumsily, as 'poetry of loss and chaos'. Both are species of what we might prefer to call by the more general term of 'war poetry', since both deal with military subjects.

However, they can be differentiated further as follows. The second type of poem lays a much heavier emphasis on the sufferings endured by war's innocent victims (butchered, mutilated or enslaved). The first concerns itself more with both the heroism on the one hand and the privations on the other of the common soldier: frequently driven many hundreds of miles away from home, while defending China's northern borders against nomadic invaders and would-be invaders.

Border poetry can trace its origins right back to the *Shijing* or *Classic of Poetry* (Zhao dynasty: more specifically, 11th–7th centuries BCE); though it was not until the fifth century CE poet Bao Zhao that it really came into its own as a distinct genre[3]. 'Poetry of loss and chaos' is more recent, in that it is particularly associated with the genocidal Mongol invasions of the thirteenth century; though one can add with some certainty that it in its turn derives from earlier poems, such as those written by Du Fu, and other Tang poets.

11

These were poems that bore witness to the seismic disaster of the An Lushan rebellion (755-763), a catastrophe that well-nigh tore the Tang dynasty apart in the mid-eighth century.

Another way to distinguish these two genres is to state (a little more hesitantly) that *sangluan* poems nearly always tend to be written by eyewitnesses and participants, whereas this is only sometimes true of border poems.

As to the extent whereby either genre can be thought of as something approaching what we in the West consider to be 'protest poetry', that is problematic. Some border poems (as in the case of the Ming loyalist Gu Yanwu) were certainly made use of to complain about wars being waged at the time of composition. However, as was customary with Chinese literature that dared to criticize a contemporary emperor or dynasty, the action of the poem was always pushed back to some much earlier era (Gu Yanwu's poem describes a battle which took place a whole century BCE, though his readers would have suspected, with good reason, that he was actually referring to the defeat of his own Ming dynasty by the Northern Manchu invaders who founded the Qing). Some *sangluan* poems either implicitly or explicitly heap opprobrium on military incompetence, cruelty or cowardice.

But much Chinese war poetry is very far from critical. What is interesting about the two relatively early war poems from that great poet Ruan Ji, as has been pointed out by Stephen Owen (*The Poetry of Ruan Ji and Xi Kang*, Boston / Berlin, 2017, pp. 15-16), is that the second of them already seems closer to that famous quotation of Wilfred Owen's: "My subject is war, and the pity of war", while the first is a conventional gung-ho paean to military prowess. This anthology, I have to admit, is somewhat biased against the second category, though a few such have necessarily been included.

The border peoples with whom Han Chinese living in the north or north-west regions (whether merchants, soldiers, or diplomats) had dealings, were many, and ethnically varied. The 'southern tribes of the Huai' and the northern 'Xianyun' were the twin enemies recognized by the Classic of Poetry. 'Xianyun' seems to have meant irrespectively everyone north of the various Han Chinese states in existence at that time. By the time of the Han the generic term in use was 'Xiongnu'. In subsequent dynasties, as different tribal peoples were distinguished, the names began to multiply: Khitan, Jurchen, Qiang, Uighur, Tangut, Mongols (to use a more recent Western nomenclature). The first two of these invaded large areas of North China and established two Chinese dynasties of their own, the Liao and the Jin respectively. The Mongols, of course, conquered the whole of China in the thirteenth century, and founded the Yuan. A generic term for all such foreign nations was 胡 hú, translated as 'barbarian' or 'nomad'. Something approaching horror was felt by the Han Chinese at these alien peoples' lack of any fixed abode, moving across the steppes as they did, in company with the herds they tended – and living indeed in such close proximity with these animals that they themselves could seem to outsiders almost bestial at times. But along with that initial repulsion, there was also a real and deepening fascination with their 'otherness': their strange but colourful customs, clothing, hairstyles, cuisine, music and dancing. This can be seen in the pictorial art of the Han and the Tang, and it sometimes comes through in their poetry as well. But 'otherness' interpreted as 'savagery' or 'barbarism' has always been how 'civilized' peoples choose to define their own 'superior' identity: Chinese and Romans then, British, French, Germans and Americans more recently.

To write with something approaching relish about the 'savage' and exotic customs of the northern and north-western barbarians, of the bleak terrain they inhabited, the harsh weather that frontier troops had to endure, and of the glory of riding into battle against hopeless odds, might seem to us a very 'Romantic' thing to do. But of course romantic poetry and painting is much older and more widespread than the label 'Western Romanticism' would lead us to believe. Many border poets had never actually visited the remote and colourful places they imagined, though they may have known others who had. My little anthology includes the full range, from what one can only call 'creative variations on a theme' by elegant and effete literati safely ensconced at court in the southern capital (e.g. the piece entitled 'Watering My Horse...' written by Chen Shubao, the last emperor of the sixth century Chen dynasty), to much grittier and more realistic accounts, some of them actually written on campaign and others upon a veteran's return. One thinks of the Tang poets Gao Shi, Cen Shen, and Li Yi who are often praised for the fact that in their border poems they wrote not merely according to literary convention but also from direct personal experience, or of Yelü Chucai, who famously travelled far beyond the north-west frontier while accompanying Genghis Khan as one of his aides[4].

Certain place-names, well-worn poetic formulae and characteristic images return again and again. The bleak and barren terrain, the inclement weather – icy blasts of wind, snow-blizzards one moment and sandstorms the next – the music of the steppes, reed-pipes sounding strange melodies across the frozen wasteland, troops setting out from some barracks on the Wall, never to return, the whitened piles of bones they leave behind after their deaths in battle, the widows and orphans pining for them thousands of miles away... all powerful stuff, though a little of this can go a long way, and there are so many hundreds and hundreds of such poems to choose from that it becomes increasingly hard for the translator to choose. I've avoided many of the most famous contenders (including several of those mentioned in the previous paragraph) since other translators have already done them ample justice. I preferred in the main to concentrate either on those who have never been previously translated, or on those who were writing at the time of the Mongol invasions, a period in which I'm particularly interested at present. Their poems move away from conventional border poetry into eyewitness sāngluàn poetry, as the reader will discover.

During that same Yuan dynasty, a certain scholar and poet, Yang Weizhen, 楊維楨 (1296-1370), is said to have fashioned a flute from an old iron sword. It played the softest music and accompanied him on his wanderings, perhaps providing some small consolation for his lack of employment. (The Mongols mistrusted the whole mandarin class, and preferred to entrust government posts to people from their own ethnic background.) Yang loved this instrument so much that he gave himself the soubriquet 'The Iron Flute Daoist' (tiědí Dàorén 鐵笛道人).There is a famous painting in the Shanghai Museum called 'The Iron Flute' that illustrates this anecdote. It has been attributed to the Ming painter Wu Wei, though American scholars believe it to be a late Qing forgery.

14

Out of the discord of war we humans can still conjure up sweet music: hence the title of this anthology.

Three war poems by the writer who is arguably China's greatest poet, Du Fu, have been included, though none of them strictly belongs to the genres mentioned above. (Those that do – and there are several famous examples – have already been brilliantly translated by others.) The approach taken in the poems I've chosen is, by contrast, subtler and more oblique. 'Insomniac Night' I consider one of the greatest war poems ever written, though my own translation can't hope to compete with that by Burton Watson. Starting off as what seems like just another 'nature' poem, it leads up slowly but inexorably, by means of a chain of cunningly related images, to a shattering climax. We are made to realize that the whole landscape is threatened by man's destructiveness. It is followed by two other fine poems that are probably already familiar to readers of Chinese poetry in translation via other versions, but which I have come to love so much that I felt I just had to try my hand at them as well.

In conclusion, my hope is that this little selection will at least allow the reader either to discover afresh or to re-experience in a new guise a range of compelling and dynamic voices from medieval China that speak to us not of scenes from a distant age and from faraway places, but of tragic events that we see played out on our television screens on a daily basis. For wherever there are human beings, there will unavoidably be war; and wherever there is war, there will be writers to record it.

NOTES

[1] Other translations of Sun Wu's famous treatise 兵法 bīngfǎ might be 'How to Wage War', 'Military Methodology', or just plain 'Warcraft' (as in the computer game).

[2] The very idea of an 'art' of war is paradoxical. Surely war always degenerates into madness and chaos? But in fact war is willed and organized, sometimes with great ingenuity, by statesmen and military strategists. It is, to them, nearly always considered as a regrettable but necessary extension of diplomacy 'by other means', as von Clausewitz puts it. The battlefield is often seen by such individuals as a sort of chessboard on a larger scale. Moreover, that war can be considered 'beautiful' is a shocking idea to many. Yet just think of the astonishing skill deployed by generations of craftsmen as they forged armour and weapons of great beauty

throughout the ages. Or consider the frequent comparisons made in Chinese and Japanese culture between the way in which a warrior flourishes his sword and the way a calligrapher wields his brush. Think of all those nineteenth century ladies and gentlemen armed with parasols, camp-stools and telescopes who tramped up hills in order to view a distant battlefield, whether Napoleonic or Unionist versus Confederate: colourful well-drilled uniforms moving in strict formation through fire and smoke, troops of infantry and cavalry charging, counter-charging or standing their ground in a disciplined way. Think of British civilians craning their eyes skyward to watch the murderous dogfights taking place high above them, and, yes, finding the spectacle strangely exhilarating. And, just as children enjoy fireworks and a huge bonfire on Guy Fawkes' Night, so Air Raid Wardens during the Blitz sometimes admitted to their diaries how beautiful the sight of a great city engulfed in flames could be, and so, more recently, journalists from hotel rooftops in Baghdad have described the sensual pyrotechnic beauty of American 'Shock and Awe' bombardment, when seen from a relatively safe distance.

The morality of war is similarly paradoxical. Clearly war itself is evil; unless one is a pacifist, it is seen as a necessary evil. But from time immemorial, the bravery of its combatants has rightly been celebrated. Such qualities as loyalty, courage and self-sacrifice have long been recognized as moral virtues and all of them are tempered in the furnace of the battlefield. One wonders from a cynical twenty-first century perspective whether patriotism should be added to the list. In any case, no one doubts that military heroes really do exist, though not all of them get medals. Chinese border poetry often pays tribute to the admirable behaviour exhibited by both the highest-ranking commander and the humblest most anonymous footsoldier; and contrariwise it also allows itself the occasional snort of derision at the laziness and incompetence of bad military leaders. The pity and the horror and the glory and the pointlessness of war: they are all present.

[3] At least to begin with, border poetry is nearly always a sub-genre of the ballad form (樂府 yuèfǔ). It begins with one of a range of traditional titles, which never vary in their wording. Here are the main ones: 從軍行 cóng jūn xíng 'With the Army', 關山月 guānshān yuè 'Moon on the Mountain-Passes', 塞上曲 sàishàng qǔ 'Song: On the Border', 出塞 chū sài 'Leaving the Border', 戰城南 zhàn chéng nán 'Fighting South of the Wall', 飲馬長城窟行 yìn mǎ Chángchéng kū xíng 'Watering My Horse in a Niche by the Wall'. One can see at a glance how suggestive such titles are, and can understand why so many poets felt impelled to rise to the challenge they posed. Once the title has been chosen, however, the poet then gets to play a sort of riff on this thoroughly conventional theme. Many such 'variations' when one encounters them in bulk in the anthologies are sufficiently similar to each other to become quite irritating after a while; but good poets always managed to give their versions a fresh twist of some kind.

[4] Nevertheless, it's worth adding the caveat that all these poets came to the actual frontier armed with expectations that had been coloured and informed by their reading: expectations that couldn't fail to influence what they wrote when they got there. (All I mean by this is that their imaginations had already been heavily impregnated by the thoroughly conventional and 'traditional' ballads they'd learned by heart beforehand. We see what we've been schooled to see. Just as the reader of Wordsworth can't help seeing the Lake District through Wordsworth's eyes, so the

16

poetizing Tang dynasty border soldier saw the north-western borderlands in and along the Gansu Corridor through the eyes of Southern Dynasties fantasists such as Chen Shubao and Zhang Zhengjian.)

PRONUNCIATION OF CHINESE NAMES

A poem stands or falls by its internal music; and it's important to pronounce more or less correctly the Chinese names included in these translations. Because the Chinese writing system is not primarily phonetic (in that it's very far from being alphabetic), we in the West have had to make use of a number of different transliteration systems over time. The two most popular with translators from the Anglo-Saxon camp have been the Wade-Giles system, which reigned supreme for well over half a century, and the Chinese Romanization system called pinyin, which has now effectively replaced Wade-Giles (though this Victorian relic still has its passionate defenders). Pinyin is what I use throughout this work.

Most of the names the reader will encounter here can be pronounced very much as they are spelled. Three letters in the pinyin alphabet, however, can completely flummox one at a first acquaintance: *c, q* and *x*. The Wade-Giles equivalents were much easier on the eye to a Western reader: *ts', ch'* and *hs* respectively.

So a personal name such as *Cen Shen* should be pronounced *Ts'en Shen*; the *Qin* dynasty is pronounced the *Ch'in* dynasty; a place-name like *Xianyang* should be pronounced *Hsien-yang,* and the *Xianyun* tribes are the *Hsien-yün* (these glosses employ the Wade-Giles method, and they all work very well).

(We Mandarin speakers are always amused at the heavy weather Western journalists and news broadcasters make of the Chinese premier's surname *Xi*. Sometimes it sounds like the name given to the letter 'g', sometimes like the first two phonemes of the word 'cheese'. In fact it should be pronounced 'Hsi': the English word 'sea' spoken with a very faint lisp (thank you again, Professors Wade and Giles).

17

TRANSLATION METHODS

My practice as a translator varies: the first objective has to be to make a poem that works in English. (I know this is a form of words that greatly irritates many other translators, but I remain unapologetic, since I judge its meaning to be pretty transparent at a first glance, at least in terms of 'ordinary common sense' – itself a phrase that likewise begs a lot of questions.) The second is to use, wherever possible or wherever appropriate, as few English syllables as I can, so as to reproduce, however faintly, the peculiar concision of Chinese classical grammar. However, notice those two qualifying phrases. Occasionally I have had to expand the original a little, in order to incorporate into any lines that required this treatment what would otherwise be ponderous academic footnotes (see below). And in one or two other cases I've amplified a line or several lines purely in order to make the poem 'work' in English, either in terms of its meaning, or of its style:[1] a perilous procedure, and one that calls to mind George Steiner's caveat: "As with a sea-shell, the translator can listen strenuously but mistake the rumour of his own pulse for the beat of the alien sea." A rendering of this kind moves towards what is sometimes called an 'imitation': something earlier generations of poets frequently indulged in, with great success (think of the Augustans). However, the translations that have pleased me most (for what it's worth) are always those that combine the closest fidelity to every character and binome in the original with the fewest words in English, while still 'working' as stand-alone poems in English.

Often I've employed the traditional 'grid', with the hanzi (Chinese characters) in the first row, one per cell, the pinyin below, and the English

---

[1] With older poems I've occasionally opted for something very close to the alliterative accentual-syllabic forms that we associate with our own medieval period (one that started much later than the Chinese 'Middle Ages') – in one case I've even inserted a few end-rhymes, a practice I normally deplore. This inevitably results in a little of the 'padding' that so weighs down and at the same time enervates the Victorian translations of that great Chinese scholar Herbert Giles; though he was making use of late Romantic verse-forms and the poetic diction that went with them: which encouraged a rather different kind of distortion.

in the third row. And underneath this grid (which only provides a literal skeleton) come all the explanatory footnotes, both Chinese and English, from whatever sources are available, if any – and if not, then from my own investigations. A single line or even a single phrase can take a week or more to decipher. At other times, if the source-text is more immediate and 'transparent' I've been a little less rigorous. In either case what usually happens next is that I need a mulling-over period of days or weeks, during which possible solutions to various lines will pop up at different times during the day (and sometimes late at night, or even in the small hours, when you wake up and find that some new arrangement of words has just occurred inside your head while you were sleeping). Finally the whole translation's first draft can come in a rush. But even then, a lot of subsequent tweaking is often required until it meets with my approval.

One occasional technique mentioned above for which no apology is needed: sometimes the translator incorporates what might have otherwise been a 'learned contextual footnote' into the body of the poem. (If the incomparable David Hinton gets away with this sort of thing, then so can I.) Cui Hao's somewhat starstruck paean to his youthful hunting-companion mentions in its very first line that Wang Weigu is already Commander of the Yulin Guard. But 'Yulin' (which translates, not very helpfully as 'Feathered Forest') means nothing to a Western reader. So I've just glossed it as 'Imperial Guard'. The first line of Gu Yanwu's 'On the Border' is an example of this sort of 'footnote expansion'. The Chinese text simply provides us with a three character phrase, 趙信城 'Zhaoxin city'; 'Xiongnu stronghold sacked' is how I've endeavoured to 'unpack' it. A whole episode from the Han war against the Xiongnu is conjured up by this richly associative place-name. The Xiongnu tribe of 'barbarians' was decisively beaten in the Battle of Mobei in 119 BC. Zhaoxin had been their stronghold in the Orkhon Valley beneath the Khangai Mountains. I've tried to compress this story into five syllables. 'Majesty, magnanimous and merciful' is a direct quote from Sima Qian's *Records of the Grand Historian*: a chapter in which a Han general tries to persuade a local king who has joined the Xiongnu to return to the Han emperor against whom he has rebelled. I suspect the phrase is as ironical in Gu Yanwu's poem as it is there. An added layer of complexity is provided, of course, by the poet's own contemporary historical context (see the relevant passage in the main body of my Introduction above).

My sources have sometimes been poetic texts and dictionaries in my own library – particularly, to begin with, the Mathews dictionary (much-maligned in recent decades, though many of us who used it before anything better became available still regard it with affection) – and subsequently the Grand Ricci, Paul Kroll's indispensable *A Student's Dictionary of Classical and Medieval Chinese* and the Taiwanese 中文大辭典 zhongwen da cidian, as well as a wide range of Chinese anthologies and editions of particular poets; but also many online sources, such as the excellent online zdic.net, the Quan Tangshi, Quan Songci and Quan Yuanqu websites provided by xysa.com and the astonishing sou-yun.com anthology of the full range of classical Chinese poets. I've also been fortunate enough to have had access over the years to the richly-stocked library of the School of Oriental and African Studies in Bloomsbury.

SOME CHINESE DYNASTIES

221-206 BCE	QIN (Ch'in) Dynasty	The 'First Emperor' (he unified the country) Capital: Chang'an, present-day Xi'an Qin Shihuangdi dies, 210 BCE.
206 BCE-220 CE	HAN Dynasty	Capitals: 1) Chang'an 2) Luoyang
220-589 CE	Six Dynasties Period (includes famous "Three Kingdoms")	Period of disunity and instability following the fall of the Han; Buddhism introduced to China
618-906 CE	TANG (T'ang) Dynasty	Capitals: Chang'an and Luoyang WANG WEI LI BO DU FU BAI JUYI
960-1279	SONG (Sung) Dynasty	Capitals: 1) Bianjing (present-day Kaifeng) 2) Lin'an (present-day Hangzhou) SU DONGPO [SU SHI]
907-1125 and 1115-1234	Liao and Jin dynasties	Northern 'barbarian' conquest dynasties by the Khitan and Jurchen tribes respectively*
1279-1368	YUAN Dynasty	The reign of the Mongol empire; Capital: Dadu (present-day Beijing)
1368-1644	MING Dynasty	Re-establishment of rule by a Han Chinese emperor; Capitals: Nanjing and Beijing
1644-1912	QING (Ch'ing) Dynasty	Reign of the Manchus (another 'barbarian' conquest dynasty); Capital: Beijing
1912-1949	Republic Period	Capitals: Beijing, Wuhan, and Nanjing
1949-present	People's Republic of China	Capital: Beijing

* Chinese dynasty charts traditionally ignore both dynasties, since in the eyes of many Chinese historians they lacked 'the Mandate of Heaven', and were ruled by non-Han Chinese emperors. To a Western observer, this seems wholly illogical: why include the Yuan and Qing dynasties, then?

21

THE IRON FLUTE
War Poems from
Ancient and Medieval China

FEWER AND FEWER

(Songs of the States: 36)

fewer and fewer …
        if we could just go home!
the Leader knows:
        he's why we're all dew-dabbled
fewer and fewer …
        if we could just go home!
it's our Leader needs us:
        he's why we're mired in mud.

式微

式微式微胡不歸
微君之故胡為乎中露
式微式微胡不歸
微君之躬胡為乎泥中

PLUCK RUSTY FERN

(Minor Odes: 167)

pluck rusty fern, pluck rusty fern,
    pluck it as it's sprouting:
homeward bound, oh homeward bound,
    when the year's on the turn –
no home and hearth to go to now,
    thanks to the Xianyun:
nowhere now to settle down,
    thanks to the Xianyun

pluck rusty fern, pluck rusty fern,
    pluck it when it's soft:
homeward bound, oh homeward bound,
    heartsore and weary –
poor hearts pinched and parched,
    we thirst and we hunger;
border-duties still not done
    still no news sent home

pluck rusty fern, pluck rusty fern,
    pluck it now it's hardened:
homeward bound, oh homeward bound
    when October comes –
the king's affairs unfinished:
    no chance for us of respite –
such bitter pangs we suffer:
    set out but don't return

what fancy flower is that?
    the blossom of the cherry
what equipage is that?
    that's a great lord's chariot –
his war-chariot made ready:
    harnessed, his four chargers …
how could we settle down?
    in one month three engagements

采薇

采薇采薇，薇亦作止。曰歸曰歸，歲亦莫止。靡室靡家，玁狁之故。不遑啟居，玁狁之故。

采薇采薇，薇亦柔止。曰歸曰歸，心亦憂止。憂心烈烈，載飢載渴。我戍未定，靡使歸聘。

采薇采薇，薇亦剛止。曰歸曰歸，歲亦陽止。王事靡盬，不遑啟處。憂心孔疚，我行不來。

彼爾維何，維常之華。彼路斯何，君子之車。戎車既駕，四牡業業。豈敢定居，一月三捷。

harnessed, his four chargers,
      his stallions so sturdy –
our leader borne behind them,
      underlings to flank him …
those stallions so sturdy,
      bow-nocks of horn, fish-scale
  quiver,
ever on the watch now:
      the Xianyun probe and harry

back then we sallied forth
      and the willow trees were stirring;
now on our return
      thick snow-flurries afflict us:
our progress home is slow,
      we thirst and we hunger,
heartsore and weary –
      no one to know our sufferings …

FROM THE SHIJING (Zhao Dynasty)

駕彼四牡四牡騤騤君子所依小人所腓四牡翼翼象弭魚服豈不日戒玁狁孔棘

昔我往矣楊柳依依今我來思雨雪霏霏行道遲遲載渴載飢我心傷悲莫知我哀

27

THE 'SEVEN SORROWS': 1

our Western Capital
          collapsed into chaos
wolves and tigers
          have torn it apart
once more escaping
          my Central Plain homeland
Jingzhou my refuge –
          savage asylum:

confronted by grief-stricken
          kinfolk's keening
fetched back by friends
          who clutch at my clothes

I push through the gate –
          desolation surrounds me
white bones, strewn cadavers
          cover the ground …
beside the roadway
          starving widows
let go of their children
          abandoned in bushes

hearing their wailing
          they turn and look back
shed tear after tear
          but cannot return
"I'm off to die somewhere –
          we can't both survive …"

unable to bear this
>I drive my steeds on
I climb Baling Mound
>(a good emperor's tomb)
turn my head round
>gaze back at Chang'an

I know what he meant
>that poet of old
who wrote *'Falling Springs'*
>(Yellow Springs of the Dead)

and venting deep sighs
>my poor heart is torn

WANG CAN (177-217)

七哀詩三首　王粲

西京亂無象豺虎方遘患復棄中國去遠身適荊蠻
親戚對我悲朋友相追攀出門無所見白骨蔽平原
路有飢婦人抱子棄草間顧聞號泣聲揮涕獨不還
未知身死處何能兩相完驅馬棄之去不忍聽此言
南登霸陵岸回首望長安悟彼下泉人喟然傷心肝

border towns breeding
      hearts that are bitter
– worse for those
      who've been here before:
ice and snow
      to scour your skin
savage winds
      whipped up without pause

not a soul to be seen
      for hundreds of miles
bushes and grasses
      that no one helps grow
climbing the ramparts
      watch-towers in view
light-fluttering dancers:
      flags hoisted aloft

one who wanders
      can't cast a look back –
once through that gate
      stop thinking of home …
sons and brothers
      hauled off as slaves
of weeping and wailing
      there can be no end

no 'happy land' left
      anywhere on earth
why do we linger
      down here so long?
do they suffer at all
      those bugs on the knotweed?
asking no questions
      they scurry to and fro

WANG CAN (177-217)

七哀詩三首　王粲

邊城使心悲昔吾親更之冰雪截肌膚風飄無止期
百里不見人草木誰當遲登城望亭燧翩翩飛戍旗
行者不顧反出門與家辭子弟多俘虜哭泣無已時
天下盡樂土何為久留茲蔘蟲不知辛去來勿與諮

30

1

"no warrior fiercer: his one wish?
　　　　　win over the wilds
his chariot driven onward
　　　　　on farflung campaigns –
obeying all orders
　　　　　forgetful of self
slung over his shoulder
　　　　　a good bow called 'Crowcaw'
flash of his breastplate
　　　　　like sparkling starlight
reckless in danger
　　　　　death lifts sky-souls aloft
why strive to stay alive
　　　　　when rushing to the front?
his fealty will linger
　　　　　through a hundred generations
his virtues a warranty
　　　　　his good name will flourish
posterity to bless him
　　　　　a constant memory his courage!"

詠懷詩十三首　其五十三　阮籍

壯士何慷慨志欲威八荒驅車遠行役受命念自忘良弓挾烏號明甲有精光臨難不顧生身死魂飛揚豈為全軀士效命爭戰場忠為百世榮義使令名彰垂聲謝后世氣節故有常

2

when young I studied swordplay
  surpassing ancient masters with my skill

with finesse I sundered rainbows
  made myself a mighty name
    ahead of all my peers ...

deserts stretched before me:
  I brandished high my blade

I took my horse to drink
  through China's nine regions

gallantly the banners flew
  drums and gongs the only din I heard

but as for military matters:
  they now just sadden me –

  bitter grief and pity now arise

I think back over my past years:
  prick of conscience springing up within ...

RUAN JI (210-263)

詠懷詩十三首　其四十七　阮籍

少年學擊刺
妙伎過曲城
英風截雲霓
超世發奇聲
揮劍臨沙漠
飲馬九野坰
旗幟何翩翩
但聞金鼓鳴

軍旅令人悲
烈烈有哀情
念我平常時
悔恨從此生

32

HARD ROAD

who hasn't seen lads
   lusty and mettlesome:
      first you enlisted,
then left for the wars –
   now white-haired vagabonds
      rootless and roofless

heading home never:
   where you first lived
      fades further away
night after night
   day after day
      all news of kinfolk

cut off forever
   countered by rivers
      by peak after peak
north winds howl bleakly
   white clouds skirl by
      screaking of reedpipes

scrannel and keen
   to pierce through this frosty
      frontier sky
you've only to hear it
   and your grief will grow
      but there's nothing for it

what unpicks the past?
   you clamber up high
      to gaze out beyond
soon you'll die trampled
   by hooves of the nomads
      no way of finding

your family at last
    male offspring fated
        to ride a rough road
who would want sons?
    sorrows unending
        sigh after sigh

BAO ZHAO (414?-466)

擬行路難十八首　其一十四　鮑照

君不見少壯從軍去白首流離不得還
故鄉窅窅日夜隔音塵斷絕阻河關朔
風蕭條白雲飛胡笳哀急邊氣寒聽此
愁人兮奈何登山遠望得留顏將死胡
馬跡寧見妻子難男兒生世轗軻欲何
道綿憂摧抑起長嘆

34

IN IMITATION OF THE BALLAD 'OUT FROM THE NORTH GATE OF JI'

from forts on the frontier
   winged missives are issued
      beacon fires flitting
         across to Xianyang
cavalry garrisoned
   in Guanwu –
      to reinforce Shuofang,
         footsoldiers billeted

keen autumn stiffening
   bowstring and bamboo stave
      barbarian warriors
         stubborn as ever
the emperor grasps his
   sword-pommel in fury –
      farflung envoys
         exchange meaning glances

one by one soldiers
   climb boulder-strewn paths
      in single file traversing
         bridges hung high
drums, pipes pulsate
   with Han people's passions
      frontierfrosts mantling
         pennants and plate-mail

sudden blasts hurling
   themselves against border-forts
      flung up from nowhere
         sandstorms come whirling
horsehairs that stiffen
   like spines on a hedgehog
      horntipped bows
         too rigid to bend

in times of great peril:
    the upright and pure
        disorder, upheaval:
            the valiant, the true
to lay down your life
    for a glorious leader –
        to die for your country:

    a noble oblation

Bao Zhao (414?-466)

代出自薊北門行　　鮑照

羽檄起邊亭烽火入咸陽徵騎屯廣武分兵救朔方
嚴秋筋竿勁虜陣精且強天子按劍怒使者遙相望
雁行緣石徑魚貫度飛梁簫鼓流漢思旌甲被胡霜
疾風沖塞起沙礫自飄揚馬毛縮如蝟角弓不可張
時危見臣節世亂識忠良投軀報明主身死為國殤

WATERING MY HORSE IN A NICHE OF THE WALL
   (Ballad)

my charger in an alien land
          – these mountain flowers that glow by night!
no herd nearby, it whinnies at its reflection
          – catching at fresh scents carried by the wind
colours of moonlight lick at the Great Wall's dark
          – along the frontier autumn voices mingle
you'll send what tribute to the Son of Heaven?
          – your own hide wrapping a corpse from the front!

CHEN SHUBAO (553-604)

飲馬長城窟行　陳叔寶

征馬入他鄉山花此夜光
離群嘶向影因風屢動香
月色含城暗秋聲雜塞長
何以酬天子馬革報疆場

FALLING SNOW

autumn now over, the nomads burst through:
a thousand miles of low cloud louring

snows go dark as barbarian sands;
ice as bright as moon on the Han

silver the watchtowers in the steep passes
jade-green the gigantic sweep of the Wall

our fluttering banners and flags have all fallen
our names are a blank to the High Son of Heaven

LU ZHAOLIN (c. 635-689)

雨雪曲　盧照鄰

虜騎三秋入關云万里平
雪似胡抄暗冰如漢月明
高關銀為關長城玉作城
節旄零落盡天子不知名

37

THE BLACK-MANED BAY
(Ballad)

glitter of this bay's gold saddle –
      after countless battles, see it enter Gaolan
wind more cutting through these frontier gates –
      waters colder by this never-ending Wall
darkness and snow: your bridle's clink-clink-clink –
      mountain after mountain, your muzzle spouting foam
never hanging back from crossing desert wastes –
      who will ever staunch this endless flow of blood?

    Lu Zhaolin (*c.* 635-689)

横吹曲辭 · 紫騮馬　盧照鄰

不雪塞騮
辭暗門馬
橫鳴風照
絕珂稍金
漢重急鞍
流山長轉
血長城戰
幾噴水入
時玉正皐
幹難寒蘭

FIGHTING SOUTH OF THE WALLS

our general's set off from the Wall
    the tribal chieftain's at Wutan
nomad reedpipes screeching
    northward of Goose Gate

      both wings spread protectively
        south of Dragon City
      carved bows twist and turn by night
        at dawn we loose our cavalry

holding back by day
    then fighting to the death

    Lu Zhaolin (*c.* 635-689)

戰城南　盧照鄰

應雕笳將
須弓喧軍
駐夜雁出
白宛門紫
日轉北塞
為鐵陣冒
待騎翼頓
戰曉龍在
方參城烏
酣驛南貪

MOON ON THE MOUNTAIN-PASSES

borderlands' immensity:
   reaching (eastwards, unimpeded)
               Dolmen Peak
yet still the nomads balk us
   westwards battering Qilian

love-longing travels for a thousand miles
   solitary, luminous
      the moon hangs overhead

among the Altai Mountains
   moonbeams shimmer over Golden Cave
      while all brightness ends
         before Jade Gate

send tidings to my lady in her boudoir:

   tie them to the feet
     of a swan-goose flying home

LU ZHAOLIN (*c.* 635-689)

關山月　盧照鄰

塞坦通碣石虜障抵祁連
相思在萬里明月正孤懸
影移金岫北光斷玉門前
寄言閨中婦時看鴻雁天

autumn winds rush by
           nomad steeds flash past
city walls all sealed
           troops lost in sudden sallies
into his temple goes the Son of Heaven
           out from the Gates of Doom his generals plunge
pell-mell they press towards the Yi and Luo
           horses and chariots by the tens of thousands
striking camp beside the Yellow River
           morale unbroken charging in broad daylight
their whole lives dreaming of the two-edged sword
           selflessly the scholar's brush laid by
southward a lone moon climbs above the Han
           northward thick clouds cluster in Dai County
know well the tactics of those ancient heroes
           never forget the ancient arts of war
sweep evil from the world a thousand miles –
           better than sweeping clean your one small room

                    Liu Xiyi (*c.* 651-*c.* 680)

從軍行　劉希夷

秋天風颯颯群胡馬行疾
嚴城晝不開伏兵暗相失
天子廟堂拜將軍凶門出
紛紛伊洛道戎馬幾萬匹
軍門壓黃河兵氣沖白日
平生懷仗劍慷慨即投筆
南登漢月孤北走代雲密
近取韓彭計早知孫吳術
丈夫清萬里誰能掃一室

TWO 'BORDER POEMS'

1: GOING UP TO THE BORDER

locusts churr in the naked mulberry groves:
        September on the Xiao Pass road
frontier-treks: forever to and fro
        everywhere the same bleached reeds and grass
old-time itinerants from You and Bing ...
        long since crumbled into dust and sand
roving freebooters – why follow their example?
        swashbucklers bragging of their black-maned bays!

2: COMING BACK FROM THE BORDER

horses watered at the ford: fall floods
        icy water; kniving wind
sun just sinking under sand-flats –
        as dusk deepens, Lintao's still distinct
those ancient campaigns on the Wall –
        all confident their nerve would hold
days ground to yellow dust ...
        white bones strewn among the tangled whin ...

WANG CHANGLING (*c.* 690-*c.* 756)

黃塵足今古白骨亂蓬蒿
昔日長城戰咸言意氣高
平沙日未沒黯黯見臨洮
飲馬渡秋水水寒風似刀

莫學遊俠兒矜誇紫騮好
從來幽並客皆共塵沙老
出塞入塞寒處處黃蘆草
蟬鳴空桑林八月蕭關道

塞下曲二首　王昌齡

41

CROSSING THE BORDER

Qin moonlight bright on Han-built fort
They've marched a thousand miles: no going home
If Dragon City's Li Guang came back here
Those nomads wouldn't push through mountain passes

    WANG CHANGLING (*c.* 690-*c.* 756)

BOUDOIR PANGS

young wife at her window
    untouched by sorrow
        spruced up for spring
            in her bright green boudoir
suddenly sees
    at the side of the road
the farewell willow's
        freshest hues …

        kniving pangs:

        why did I pack him off to war
          in search of a title?

    WANG CHANGLING (*c.* 690-*c.* 756)

不教胡馬渡陰山
但使龍城飛將在
萬里長征人未還
秦時明月漢時關

出塞　王昌齡

悔教夫婿覓封侯
忽見陌頭楊柳色
春日凝妝上翠樓
閨中少婦不知愁

閨怨　王昌齡

THE SQUADDIE'S ANCIENT SONG

by day you climb the slope to scan the warning-beacons
come twilight near Jiaohe you water horses

       some squaddie sounds the night-watch,
          bangs his mess-kit gong –

in a sandstorm blackout
   a captive princess vents her many secret sorrows
      by playing on the *pipa*

ten thousand leagues from any city wall your camp
   vast deserts uniform with constant sleet and snow

          Tartar geese fly by each night
             uttering sad cries
         a Tartar youth sheds tears
             with both cheeks streaming

we hear that Jade Gate Pass is to be closed;
yet we're the ones who sacrifice our lives
      behind the general's light chariots

unnumbered years of warfare:
   our bones lie buried under barren skies

what a futile task:
     and all to heap Han tables high

      with foreign grapes

Li Qi (690-751)

相和歌辭

從軍行　李頎

白日登山望烽火黃昏飲馬傍交河行人刁斗風砂暗公主琵琶幽怨多

野雲萬裡無城郭雨雪紛紛連大漠胡雁哀鳴夜夜飛胡兒眼淚雙雙落

聞道玉門猶被遮應將性命逐輕車年年戰骨埋荒外空見蒲萄入漢家

BORDER ENVOY

driving my chariot out to the frontier –
    crossing the Juyan dependency

(puffball tossed past homeland walls;
    wild goose blown through alien skies)

        vast savanna: line of smoke lifts up
        mighty river: orb of fire slides down –

at Xiao Pass troopers tell me:
    "The General's made it to Yanran!"

WANG WEI (691?-761)

使至塞上　王維

單車欲問邊屬國過居延
征蓬出漢塞歸雁入胡天
大漠孤煙直長河落日圓
蕭關逢候吏都護在燕然

44

YINGZHOU SONG

Yingzhou's young bucks throng the steppes
    beneath the battlements soft fox-fur coats go hunting
nomad liquor never makes them drunk –
    ten years old, their sons can ride a horse

    GAO SHI (704-765)

營州歌　高適

營州少年滿原野狐裘蒙茸獵城下
虜酒千鐘不醉人胡兒十歲能騎馬

LIANGZHOU SONG

this fine wine, these goblets   of glittery pearl …
the *pipa* player astraddle his horse   demands that we drink!
Don't laugh if I'm tipsy,   sprawled on the sandy ground
how many soldiers of old   who set out to battle
    ever returned?

    WANG HAN (*fl.* 720)

涼州詞　王翰

葡萄美酒夜光杯欲
飲琵琶馬上催
醉臥沙場君莫笑古
來征戰幾人回

he's thirty years old: the Imperial Guard's Commander
    – daily border battles (his life's on the line) …
spring winds flatten these thin grasses
    as he rides out hunting, lithe and spry …
look to the arrows at each shoulder's quiver –
    twang of our newly tightened bows –
the shot elk enters a deep ravine
    so our horses can drink,
        splash into desolate springs:
mounted both, we share a cup of wine,
    eke out our lives with slices of fresh meat;
while watching one another's back,
    when can we properly water our steeds?
        all kinds of savages
            plundering distant Yan
far beacons blazing without stint,
    barbarian hooves raise dust up to the sky
safeguarding the north-east,
    we constantly push onwards
        to end the fighting and preserve the city-walls

we serve our country, strive to keep it safe
    since ancient times we all make common cause

CUI HAO (704-754)

贈王威古　崔顥

三十羽林將，出身常事邊。
春風吹淺草，獵騎何翩翩。
插羽兩相顧，鳴弓新上弦。
射麋入深谷，飲馬投荒泉。
馬上共傾酒，野中聊割鮮。
相看未及飲，雜虜寇幽燕。
烽火去不息，胡塵高際天。
長驅救東北，戰解城亦全。
報國行赴難，古來皆共然。

INSOMNIAC NIGHT

the chill of bamboo
        seeps into my bed
a wilderness moon
        spills over the quad
dense dew trickles
        perfect tiny droplets
sparse stars glimmer, then
        gutter into gloom
self-sparking glow-worms
        flitter through the dark
waterfowl keen
        to each other half asleep …
war and its weapons
        impend over all:
grief blanks out
        as the cool night passes

Du Fu (712-770)

萬　重　暗　竹
事　露　飛　涼　　倦
干　成　螢　侵　　夜
戈　涓　自　臥
裏　滴　照　內　　杜
空　稀　水　野　　甫
悲　星　宿　月
清　乍　鳥　滿
夜　有　相　庭
徂　無　呼　隅

47

VIEW IN SPRING

the country crumbles:	mountains and rivers remain
city in springtime:	grass and trees grow wild
a time of troubles:	even the flowers shed tears
pain of apartness:	flown bird startles the heart
beacons burning	three whole months
a letter from home	– worth a mint of money
scratched my white hair	*till it's worn quite thin*
not enough left	*to hold one pin*

Du Fu (712-770)

春望　杜甫

國破山河在城春草木深
感時花濺淚恨別鳥驚心

SCANNING THE WILDERNESS

cloudless autumn –
　　　　yet furthest sight is baffled
the more remote
　　　　the more thick shadows gather …
distant rivers
　　　　blur into the sky –
thick mist shrouds
　　　　a lonely fort
a gust of wind
　　　　sets sparse leaves a-quiver
sunlight sinks
　　　　behind the far-flung hills
a single crane flops home –
　　　　why so late?
crows cluster on black boughs
　　　　as twilight falls

Du Fu (712-770)

野望　杜甫

清秋望不極迢遞起曾陰
遠水兼天淨孤城隱霧深
葉稀風更落山迥日初沈
獨鶴歸何晚昏鴉已滿林

FIVE FRONTIER SONGS

I

gilded arrows
    fletched with falcon feathers –
        the general's gonfalon,
            embroidered, swallowtailed …
standing alone,
    he bellows his command:
        a thousand soldiers answer
            with a single cry

II

dark woods –
    breeze that makes the grasses bristle –
        at nightfall, says the legend,
            General Li Guang draws his bow …
dawn comes,
    he hunts for his white fletching:
        fails to find it
            in the stone it sank right through …

III

a moonless sky:
    wild geese flying high
        all through the night
            the Khan is on the run
longed-for light cavalry
    hasten in pursuit –
        our swords and arrows
            swallowed up in snow …

IV

our troops' tents
    sprawl out across the steppes
        widespread revelry and feasting
            tribute paid for routing nomad tribes
wild dancing and drunkenness:
    armour's gold-glitter
        and drumming's deep thunder
            makes hills and rivers shake

V

muster bowmen; laud the hawk
    make your prowess known
        fly after foxes,
            flush pheasants from their coverts
sweep clean, sweep clean
    those ancient hills –
      until your enemies
        are all wiped out

Lu Lun (748-799?)

塞下曲四首　盧綸

鷲翎金仆姑　燕尾繡蝥弧
獨立揚新令　千營共一呼
林暗草驚風　將軍夜引弓
平明尋白羽　沒在石棱中
月黑雁飛高　單於夜遁逃
欲將輕騎逐　大雪滿弓刀
野幕敞瓊筵　羌戎賀勞旋
醉和金甲舞　雷鼓動山川
調箭又呼鷹　俱聞出世能
奔狐將逐雉　掃盡古丘陵

autumn moon so bright, so high
    shining north of Liaoyang walls

this far-flung border-pass:
    first-watch, brilliance now at the full –
gathering winds –
    moon-halo growing and growing …

sentries gazing down – sweet dreams of home
    stallions startled at the thudding of a drum

north winds bring grief to frontier grasslands
    sandstorms shrouding the nomad camp

frost makes the sword stick to its scabbard
    winds fray to shreds our upland banners …

soon, please, soon to go back to the palace –
    no more to hear the clangour
        of night-watch mess-tins!

    Bao Junhui (*fl.* 798)

關山月　鮑君徽

高高秋月明北照遼陽城塞迴光初滿風多暈更生
征人望鄉思戰馬聞鼙驚朔風悲邊草胡沙暗虜營
霜凝匣中劍風憊原上旌早晚謁金闕不聞刁斗聲

ON SIGHTING JIMEN PASS

your heart shrinks
    when you leave Yantai
        thudding drums – screak of reed-flutes
           near the general's camp

thousands and thousands of miles:
    freezing light strengthens on bright snow
        as dawn floods borderlands
           and banners flutter high

barbaric moonlight dimmed
        by flaming beacons over battlefields

coastal clouds shroud mountains
    round Jimen Pass's city

I may not be the scholar
    who once flung his pen down
        to enlist

        but I too seek
          the ribbon of renown

ZU YONG (Tang, 8th century)

望薊門　祖詠

燕臺一望客心驚
笳鼓喧喧漢將營
萬裏寒光生積雪
三邊曙色動危旌
沙場烽火連胡月
海畔雲山擁薊城
少小雖非投筆吏
論功還欲請長纓

ARROWHEAD[1]

char of ashes
    pashed bonedust
        in wet red clay

old blood spilled
    blossoms
        on the bronze

white plumes rotted,
    iron shaft rusted
        in the rains

just this wolf's
    cracked canine left:
        its three blunt points …

two steeds I've raced
    over this flatland
        searching

here by the eastern courier station
    in this tangled ditch
        on the stony field of battle

winds dilate
    as daylight narrows,
        bleak stars blinking on

cloud-skeins unfurl
    banners of black rain:
        night engulfs me

長平箭頭歌　李賀

漆灰骨末丹水沙淒淒古血生銅花
白翎金竿雨中盡直餘三脊殘狼牙
我尋平原乘兩馬驛東石田蒿塢下
風長日短星蕭蕭黑旗雲濕懸空夜
左魂右魄啼肌瘦酪瓶倒盡將羊炙
蟲棲雁病蘆筍紅回風送客吹陰火
訪古汍瀾收斷鏃折鋒赤璺曾劇肉
南陌東城馬上兒勸我將金換篆竹

53

and the starved shades keening
    lift and dip
        to right and left[2]

swooping down
    they gulp curds from my pitcher
        guzzle my roast mutton

gnat-swarms settle; set geese screeching
    as reeds and bamboo-shoots
        are flushed with final red

the gale whirls phantom
    firedrakes round me
        to guide me on my way

I've tracked down this ancient lamentation
    to bring it to an end:
        one broken arrowhead

this stark snapped barb
    I take away
        once stuck in living meat

I gain South Street:
    beside the eastern wall
        a boy on horseback

bids me barter
    my metal relic
        for a bamboo tray[3]

    LI HE (791-817)

nomad horns reel in
   cold northern winds
      Thistle Gate a-shimmer
         white as rushing water
these skies lap up
   the road to Kokonor –
      along the battlements
         a thousand miles of moonlight
banners drenched
   by dewfall
      night-watches sounded out
         by ice-cold brass
barbarian armour:
   snake's interlocking scales
      horses whinny:
         the exile's green grave whitens
autumn stillness:
   the Pleiad flickers, signifying war
      on far-flung sands
         bleak wasteland of dried grasses
north of nomad tents
   is where horizons end
      rivers flowing on
         beyond all frontiers

   Li He (791–817)

塞下曲　李賀

胡角引北風
薊門白於水
天含青海道
城頭月千裡
露下旗濛濛
寒金鳴夜刻
蕃甲鎖蛇鱗
馬嘶青塚白
秋靜見旄頭
沙遠席羈愁
帳北天應盡
河聲出塞流

UIGHUR SONG: NORTHERN BORDER

Uighur gold caps throng our battlements
      Yinshan's barren mountain slopes
snowflakes float outside my tent
      moon-blanched sands beyond the fort

a tribesman's son tootles his jade pipe
      barbarian girls pace flower-strewn brocade
yet laughter's shared:
      me and my southern guest –

don't go home
      until plum-blossom falls

    WEN TINGYUN (801?-866)

敕勒歌塞北　溫庭筠

敕勒金巾貴壁陰山無歲華
帳外風飄雪瑩前月照沙
羌兒吹玉管胡姬踏錦花
卻笑江南客梅落不歸家

SEEING A FRIEND OFF EAST

dead leaves twirl and skitter
  empty barracks square

      leaving this old mountain pass,
        your heart, it swells …

Hanyang ferry:
      howling winds
Yingmen mountain:
      rising sun …

who'll still haunt the riverside
  when, from the back of beyond,
      your sole boat returns?

whenever that may be
  we'll drown our sorrows now
    by drinking deep together

    WEN TINGYUN (801?-866)

送人東游　溫庭筠

荒戌落黃葉浩然離故關
高風漢陽渡初日郢門山
江上幾人在天涯孤棹還
何當重相見樽酒慰離顏

A SONG OF DISTANT RIVERS

this year's ninth moon
    the emperor's troops
        plash through distant fords

their horses plough through sand
    wildgeese fly up alarmed

murderous chill blasts
    through empty open country:
        home-thoughts …
            so many miles away …

ramparts mantled by unending frost
    smoke from beacon fires

dry leaves
    shrill winds lamenting
        a whole world withering

not belts made from rhino hide
    nor doublets of sable-fur
        keep them warm

moonglare
    dazzling cold
        saddles worked in gold
their foes' thick dust
    flung up like mist at twilight
        veils our camp from view

remember how the Flying General
    hero of those ancient border wars
        came to Longshou countless times
yet they never hung his image
    in Unicorn Pavilion's
        Hall of Fame

in high boudoirs
   grieving women
      all still vainly gazing north

WEN TINGYUN (801?-866)

遏水謠　溫庭筠

天兵九月渡遏水馬踏沙鳴驚雁起殺氣空高萬裡情塞寒如箭傷眸子
狼煙堡上霜漫漫枯葉號風天地干犀帶鼠裘無暖色清光炯冷黃金鞍
虜塵如霧罩亭障隴首年年漢飛將麟閣無名期未歸樓中思婦徒相望

PITY THE PLOUGHMAN

name me a dynasty,
      name me a reign
            without war:
never peace
      and plenty ... chaos
            never-ending

more bones than topsoil
      turned up
            by your plough;
and still they come recruiting –
      soldiers

            seeking soldiers

WEI ZHUANG (836-910)

憫耕者　韋莊

何代何王不戰爭盡從離亂見清平
如今暴骨多於土猶點鄉兵作戍兵

ALONE ON A FRONTIER-WALL, LOOKING AT THE VIEW

lean on the battlements: look down there –
    rush of regret – a remembered town ...

frost falls on whitened reeds;
    mountains at dusk: mist makes fresh dew ...

Northern geese roost on shores of the river;
    drums set the palisades bristling with spears ...

that one crippled tree, now coloured by autumn –
    a wild song to weep at, to dampen hat-tassels ...

MA DAI (*fl.* 9th century)

邊城獨望　馬戴

聊憑危堞望倍起異鄉情
霜落蒹葭白山昏霧露生
河灘胡雁下戎壘漢鼙驚
獨樹殘秋色狂歌淚滿纓

59

A REPORT:
WHAT GOES ON IN THE BORDERLANDS

a bugle's muster-call

    shatters autumn's sparkle

as conscripts lounge at ease

    against watchtowers …

spring breezes now

    caress green burial-mounds –

a spring day sheds its brilliance

    throughout Liangzhou …

no soldiers bar the way

    across these empty wilds

each rover free to roam

    the furthest frontier

those nomads' wanderlust

    runs loose as any river

their only wish, as ever,

    to flow towards the south

ZHANG QIAO (Tang dynasty)

書邊事　張喬

調角斷清秋征人倚戌樓
春風對青塚白日落梁州
大漢無兵阻窮邊有客遊
蕃情似此水長願向南流

ON THE BORDER, REPLYING TO A FRIEND

the frontier crossed,
     boundlessly you roamed –

    when you got back,
        your hair had turned quite white

        encircled now, those nomad tribes
          (sleep in the saddle while sandstorms flail)

           grasslands all scorched, bleached –
             frozen ears can't hear cicadas cry

from here on, you'll put up with penury –
    no more prattle, please,

        till more men reach the border

            LIN KUAN (Tang dynasty)

塞上還答友人　林寬

無端遊絕塞歸鬢已蒼然
戎羯圍中過風沙馬上眠
草衰頻過燒耳冷不聞蟬
從此甘貧坐休言更到邊

61

axle-creak, wheel-clatter …
        shoving, heaving over rugged mountain-paths,
an early solitary start –
        all you hear is water-plash and -chuckle
winds rise
        night-mist scatters
moonglow brightening
        on Hua mountain-slopes
those who travel east and west:
        their hair's gone white
the Yellow River
        continuously cold and clear!
everyone you meet:
        busy, busy, busy:

you're the only one
        who's idle

LIN KUAN (Tang dynasty)

關下早行　林寬

軋軋推危轍
聽雞獨早行
風吹宿靄散
月照華山明
白首東西客
黃河晝夜清
相逢皆有事
唯我是閒情

62

ON THE BORDER

the whoosh of whistling arrows
      shot straight up a thousand feet –
   sounding even sharper

                in this tranquil windless sky …

and these blue-eyed nomad youths
      on their three hundred steeds –
   all clutching their gold bridles,
         gazing up towards the clouds …

                             LIU KAI (947-1000)

塞上　柳开

鳴骹直上一千尺天靜無風聲更乾
碧眼胡兒三百騎盡提金勒向雲看

63

dawn: haloed moonglow
      – city under siege
night: high winds
      – camp under attack

hornblasts clanging:
      icy waters shudder
bowstrings' twanging force:
      lone goose startled into flight

sharp arrowbarbs
      impale Wu breastplates
long-poled halberds
      slash and snap Chu chin-straps

      turn round – gaze back upon the battlefield

        dark and comfortless
           at dusk   mists rise

ZHAO BINGWEN (1159-1232)

回看經戰處慘淡暮煙生
利鏃穿吳甲長戈斷楚纓
角聲寒水動弓勢斷鴻驚
月暈曉圍城風高夜斫營

盧州城下　趙秉文

64

BITTER COLD

October:
> *filthy frontier weather*

our soldiers'
> *flimsy winter furs*

and is the envoy
> *bringing us new clothes or not?*

icy scales of armour:
> *long insomniac nights*

> those ministers in Chang'an:
>> warm and snug
>
> sun's high: but their red-lacquered gates
>> stay firmly shut
>
> swathed by screens and curtains
>> fold on fold –
>
> too drunk to even be aware
>> of all those shivering outside

LIU KEZHUANG (1187-1269)

重重幛箔施屏山中酒不知屏外寒
長安城中多熱官朱門日高未啟關
押衣敕使來不來夜長甲冷睡難著
十月邊頭風色惡官軍身上衣裘薄

苦寒行　劉克莊

BUILDING WALLS

incessant commotion and clamour
    of thousands of labourers' mallets
        mallets that startle poor mother earth
            with all their thwacking and thumping

everywhere clearing the villagers' land
    constructing clay-kilns belching out smoke
        spying out woodland for timber to fell
            to build up more watch-towers

days so brief
    air so keen
        gangmasters laying about them
            with white rods
hoarse voices upbraiding the workers
        like pelting wind and rain

    "the House of Han's high minister's
        obsessed about the borderlands
    building walls builds us up too
        and wins us high promotion"

long ago the wilderness
    was wide and free of walls

now warning-beacons
    file for miles
        walls must be lined with troops

but you, sir, far away, don't see
    how snaggle-toothed walls look
how soon they stick up like fish-scales

    walk all along them: empty now

        not a single soldier left

LIU KEZHUANG (1187-1269)

築城行　劉克莊

萬夫喧喧不停杵
杵聲丁丁驚后土
遍村開田起窯竈
望青斫木作樓櫓
天寒日短工役急
白棒訶責如風雨
漢家丞相方憂邊
築城功高除美官
舊時廣野無城處
而今烽火列屯戍
君不見高城藹藹
如魚鱗城中蕭疏空無人

DYING FOR YOUR COUNTRY

our army fought at midnight
      (much blood was shed)

at dawn troops gather up the fallen
      they strip each corpse of armour
before they dig its grave:
      a mass of thickly scattered burial mounds
random cairns piled up on top

– futile hanging up their names
      when tallying your dead
poor families have no salaries sent home
      orphans get no pension

sad that all these generals
      are basking in the high sun's rays –

how can they detect
      the wail of cold and cutting winds
            that summon up
                  so many thousand ghosts?

    LIU KEZHUANG (1187-269)

國殤行　劉克庄

官軍半夜血戰來平明軍中收遺骸

埋時先剝身上甲標成叢塚高崔嵬

1208: CURRENT AFFAIRS

poets in this peaceful time
　　all sporting silken
　　　　green official jackets:

but this year's treaty with the Jin
　　will cost how many bolts of silk?

no more shady willows
　　round West Lake
clustered mulberry trees
　　on all sides now

　　　　　for rearing munching silkworms

　　LIU KEZHUANG (1187-1269)

A RELATIVE IN MOURNING

desert sands
　　　　for miles and miles and miles –
　　　　　　a widow's greying hair …

your broken heart –
　　this frontier town
　　　　beneath that moon:
　　　　　　it drifts by,
　　　　　　　　shines down on the wanderer

　　YELÜ CHUCAI (1190-1244

AFTER THE EMPEROR LEFT TO TOUR EAST: JANUARY 1233

See them gallop by
   whipping their steeds
        kingfisher feathers stitched
            into their quilted robes
– bury your head in the sand
       to look at the sky!

all I know is
   north of the Yellow River
      the brigands are on their way back
and from the walls of Taicheng
   paper kites flutter and fall
      signalling, 'Help!'

… our ministers worse
than those in Xizong's reign …
when will telling the truth
      guide us back home?
autumn winds travel thousands and thousands of miles:
      all they see is one small fishing boat

YUAN HAOWEN (1190-1257)

壬辰十二月車駕東狩後即事五首其一　元好問

翠被忽忽見執鞭戴盆鬱鬱夢瞻天
隻知河朔歸銅馬又說臺城墮紙鳶
血肉正應皇極數衣冠不及廣明年
何時真得攜家去萬裡秋風一釣船

THE VIEW FROM STONE-RIDGE PASS

rattle and creak –
        careening over rock ruts –
                felt-covered wagons

this ancient pass
        still garrisoned and guarded
                by blade and bow

from strung-out encampments below
        sudden dashes of cavalry
                darken the world's red dust

those refugees
        who've donned disguise
                must take the narrow paths
                    much higher up

and as for those
        now turned to wormsmeat
                or to grains of sand

                don't waste time mourning them –

when preyed upon
        by tigers and by jackals:

        which way to turn?

And yet high up,
      cloud-clad,
            clear as jade,
                  in bluest solitude,
                        at thirty thousand feet …

Dongshan, the hermit's peak,

    still stands …

YUAN HAOWEN (1190-1257)

石嶺關書所見　元好問

軋軋旃車轉石槽
故關猶復戍弓刀
連營突騎紅塵暗
微服行人細路高
已化蟲沙休自歎
厭逢豺虎欲安逃
青雲玉立三千丈
元隻東山意氣豪

LEAVING THE CITY

In the halls of the Han
           they made sure they heard
the songs of the bard …
              days long gone – today what heroes step forward?

now in the city
        all you can see, high on the roofs,
                flocks of gold siskins

how would they know
        of the tangle of brambles that smother
                the camels of bronze?

the gods return no more
        to those who drift with the fall winds
wealth and rank are empty and bitter
        an old woman's dream of spring

you pass by Lugou again
        and again you turn
                to look back

over Feng City day
        after day the same
                weird five-coloured clouds

   YUAN HAOWEN (1190-1257)

出都二首　元好問

漢宮曾動伯鸞歌事去英雄不奈何
但見觚棱上金爵豈知荊棘臥銅駝
神仙不到秋風客富貴空悲春夢婆
行過盧溝重回首鳳城平日五雲多

72

JUNE 12TH, 1233 – CROSSING NORTH: THREE VERSES

corpses sprawled, curled up beside the road
  hordes of half-dead prisoners
    Mongol felt-topped wagons
      plunging past,
        a flood in spate …
weeping women trail
  these Uighur steeds
    for each step taken,
      who won't cast a backward glance?

behind the troops
  bundles of cheap wooden Buddhas – kindling …
    skirl of pipes, bells clanging:
      soldiers pack
        the marketplace aswirl
men of rank imprisoned,
  pillaged homes
    no one knows how many
      all year huge boats
        sailing to Kaifeng

bones stacked high like sticks of hemp
  the homeland's hacked-down mulberries, catalpas
    ferried to Longsha: how long?

this much I know: north of the Yellow River

our spirit's broken,

houses smashed –

thin smoketrails … all that's left of home

YUAN HAOWEN (1190-1257)

癸巳五月三日北渡三首　元好問

道傍僵臥滿累囚　過去旃車似水流
紅粉哭隨回鶻馬　為誰一步一回頭

隨營木佛賤於柴　大樂編鍾滿市排
虜掠幾何君莫問　大船渾載汴京來

白骨縱橫似亂麻　幾年桑梓變龍沙
隻知河朔生靈盡　破屋疏煙卻數家

hundreds of rivers and mountains   – grasses untrampled
for ten years their cavalry   darkened the walls of our capital
scan those lands to the west: no letters from Qiyang
Gansu's rivers flow to the east   freighted with our tears
sad scrubland   tangled with our soldiers' bones
the sun sets over an empty city: why shine at all?
who cries out   to the blue inhuman sky,
to ask why Chi You   forged the first weapons of war?

from the high passes
    nine tigers's piercing vision:
        nine generals from the past
            watch over these poltroons –
                their paltry strategems

the soil of Yugong's fields ... this mighty land
    home of the Han, its frontiers sealed
        as far as Heaven's Peak

blast of north wind's keening reed-flute
    plash of Wei River's icy waters
        plunging over soldiers' bones

thirty-six sharp blade-like ridges,
    reaching up to the sky
        God's Palm to protect us
            ... our empty frontiers

YUAN HAOWEN (1190-1257)

歧陽三首　元好問

百二關河草不橫十年戎馬暗秦京
岐陽西望無來信隴水東流聞哭聲
野蔓有情縈戰骨殘陽何意照空城
從誰細向蒼蒼問爭遣蚩尤作五兵

眈眈九虎護秦關懦楚孱齊機上看
禹貢土田推陸海漢家封徼盡天山
北風獵獵悲笳發渭水瀟瀟戰骨寒
三十六峰長劍在倚天仙掌惜空閑

75

WHAT THOSE GIRLS WERE SINGING ...

Wu's young ones singing
           as they trek down the road –
                    mile after mile
                              the sound of their singing

girls singing as they must,
          softened by the same shared song,
                    leaving loved fields, gathered in grief
                            at the loss of their country

day after day riders down from the north,
                piled-up clouds in battle-array:
                      steep banks of a river,
                            a long high wall ...

on countless villages
          a myriad Mongols fall:
                    government troops
                        hang back defending the city –

not enough mountain-caves,
          not enough river-boats,
                    a single horseman spurs on several thousands ...

those who survive this year,
          who knows if they'll get through the next?

blue hills of the highlands ...
                gazing south,
                    the river never ends
                            that winds round the walls of the city

willing yourself
  to follow that river –
    when it reaches the sea-bed,
      you know it'll never return

the same sand blown by the wind today
  that blew by yesterday:
    faltering feet of the female slave …
      the road stretching further and further away

… wild geese wing it together over the river
    their keening cries blend with our songs, with our tears
each autumn they come back, the wild geese,
    en route to the south –
      once over the ferry from north to south
      how many of us will return?

how still Zhuxi is: no dust stirs …
  while down there in Jiangnan: spring with its mist and rain –
so sad – today this road is flat as the river
  bristles and briars as far as the eye can see:
    no sign of life, not anywhere

before they left their fields behind
  marriage-hymns, peace and plenty:
    how they suffer now, those boys and girls!
three centuries they kept things as they'd always been:
    their sheep and kine now all desert sands

carrion birds keep guard where men once were:
　　　　torn shreds of blue cloth … old headscarves left behind
In June a wind from the south,
　　　travelling thousands of miles
　　　　to blow to dust what once was flesh and bone …

YUAN HAOWEN (1190-1257)

續小娘歌十首　元好問

吳兒沿路唱歌行十十五五和歌聲唱得小娘相見曲不解離鄉去國情

北來遊騎日紛紛斷岸長堤是陣雲萬落千村藉不得城池留著護官軍

山無洞穴水無船單騎驅人動數千直使今年留得在更教何處過明年

青山高處望南州漫漫江水繞城流願得一身隨水去直到海底不回頭

風沙昨日又今朝踏碎鴉頭路更遙不似南橋騎馬日生紅七尺係郎腰

雁雁相送過河來人歌人哭雁聲哀雁到秋來卻南去南人北渡幾時回

竹溪梅塢靜無塵二月江南煙雨春傷心此日河平路千裏荊榛不見人

太平婚嫁不離鄉楚楚兒郎小小娘三百年來涵養出卻將沙漠換牛羊

饑鳥坐守草間人青布猶存舊領巾六月南風一萬裏若為白骨便成塵

黃河千裏扼兵衝虜號分明在眼中為向淮西諸將道不須誇說蔡州功

swords and shields surround us:
                battle-slaughter's blood-stench –
while head still sits on shoulders,
                a man must follow fame

when sick, you seek a remedy:
                rest is what's required
when jaded, it's your library:
                but sleep's the best solution

the idler: head's turned by,
                eyes catch at
                        all that passes
give him just one cup,
                he's brimful of emotion

this body's only goal now:
                grow old among old mountains
me and mountain flowers:
                we understand each other

    DUAN KEJI (1196-1254)

此身定向山間老我與山英有舊盟
萬事轉頭慵挂眼一杯到手最關情
病尋藥物為開計悶引文書作睡程
四海干戈戰血腥頭皮留在更須名

排悶　段克己

outcome of those battles undecided:
   so where can I now run?
     completely futile everything I've done –
       my white hair's thin as silk …
Wang Can's, Du Fu's anecdotes about war's chaos:
   I track them both – my poor heart far behind
     who hears the wagtail from a thousand miles away?
       this magpie shivers on one moonlit branch
oh, where's the wine that Daoist sage once brewed
   that kept you sozzled for at least three years?
I'd drink and and drink drink it
    until peaceful times returned

 Wang Zhong (*fl.* 13th century)

干戈　王中

干戈未定欲何之一事無成兩鬢絲
蹤跡大綱王粲傳情懷小樣杜陵詩
鶺鴒音斷人千里烏鵲巢寒月一枝
安得中山千日酒酩然直到太平時

80

STARVELING STEED

Ever since clouds and mist
      rolled down
              into the stronghold of Sky Pass
see how the Song's twelve stables
      have decayed –

who takes pity today
      on this poor bag of bones?
yet in the sun's last rays
      how vast his shadow on the sandy shore:
          like a mountain!

GONG KAI (1222-1307)

瘦馬圖　龔開

一從雲霧降天關空盡先朝十二閑
今日有誰憐瘦骨夕陽沙岸影如山

OLD HORSE

strength all spent
      fetched back from
            fourscore battlefields
this worn out warhorse
        overtaken by old age

– hangs its head:
      – old bones once worth their weight in gold …

    its heart still hungers
        for hundreds
            and hundreds of miles

veiled its glory-days of yore
        those dusty winds

have drifted off
      – far distant now those frontier walls

short-winded its brief song:
      a hollow pot of silver

yet always it recalls
      the cries of the fallen

   HAO JING (1233-1275)

老馬　郝經

百戰歸來力不任消磨神駿老駸駸垂頭自惜千金骨伏櫪仍存萬裡心
歲月淹延官路杳風塵荏苒塞垣深短歌聲斷銀壺缺常記當年烈士吟

FIGHTING SOUTH OF THE WALL

savage fighting by our soldiers
      south of the wall's banked earthwork
horses stumbling to a standstill
      in the snow …

          and now our wall's quite lost to view

frostbitten fingers pluck at bowstrings –
      those fingers then snap off
touch icy metal
      and your skin will crack and blister

no hot meals for seven days:
      with our bare hands
         we slaughter prisoners
            to swallow their warm blood

we're promised gold
      for all the severed heads we bring
         our horses muffled,
            by night we infiltrate their lines

gloomy skies above us, darkness here below
      from our saddles hanging:
         lopped mazards streaked with tears

this second-in-command's flayed back
      bears eighty wounds
cadavers swathed in tattered banners
      heaped beside the road

we survivors all resigned to die
      shed tears beneath abandoned walls

… our general is the only one
    who's mentioned in despatches

SONG WU (1260-*c.* 1340)

戰城南　宋無

漢兵鏖戰城南窟雪深馬僵漢城沒凍指控弦指斷折寒膚著鐵膚裂
軍中七日不火食手殺降人吞熱血漢懸千金購首級將士銜枚夜深入
天愁地黑聲啾啾鞍下髑髏相對泣偏裨背負八十創破旗裹屍橫道旁
殘卒忍死哭空城露布獨有都護名

A SONG ACCOMPANIED BY STRINGS

         – pity the refugees!
human? barely even human …
   ghosts? they're barely even ghosts …
         – pity the refugees!
the men lack even homespun hempen garb;
   the women's skirts are tattered rags
         – pity the refugees!
their food is peeling bark from trees
   or grubbing grass-roots from the earth
         – pity the refugees!
by day they stumble on without cooked food,
   at night they lodge beneath the stars
         – pity the refugees!
no father's a true father to his son,
   no son's a true son to his parents
         – pity the refugees!
you just can't bear to listen to their speech,
   you just can't bear to hear their shrieks and howls
         – pity the refugees!
each morning guarantees no dusk,
   each nightfall guarantees no dawn
         – pity the refugees!
their dead already clog our roads,
   those left alive themselves close kin to ghosts
         – pity the refugees!
a woman barters for a cup of grain,
   or sells her son there for a few poor coins
         – pity the refugees!
maybe no one wants this,
   but he's now cast aside like roadside dust
         – pity the refugees!

when skies cascade down grain –
   that's when these women might survive … and only then
         – oh, pity the refugees!

ZHANG YANGHAO (1269-1329)

哀流民操　張養浩

哀哉流民為鬼非鬼為人非人哀哉流民男子無緼袍婦女無完裙哀哉流民剝樹食其皮掘草食其根哀哉流民晝行絕煙火夜宿依星辰哀哉流民父不子厭子子不親厭親鄰哀哉流民言辭不忍聽號哭不忍聞哀哉流民朝不敢保夕暮不敢保晨哀哉流民死者已滿路生者與鬼鄰哀哉流民文哀哉流民甚至不得將割愛委路塵哀哉流民何時天雨粟使女俱生存哀哉流民一女易斗粟一兒錢數

84

AN INCURABLE DISEASE

soulmates swallowed up
          in slaughter and confusion,
disaster, devastation
          as the old disease digs deeper
vain the conflict
          with all-consuming chaos,
vanished the virtuous
          sages of old
gloaming's fiery glimmer
          alarms poor refugees,
frost at first light
          reminds them of home
bowing and scraping
          for a few pecks of rice –
but this old battered besom's
          still worth a crock of gold

ZHOU TINGZHEN (1292-1379)

老病　周霆震

喪亂交遊盡艱難老病深寥寥平世策落落古人心
夕照驚岐路晨霜憶故林折腰寧五斗敝帚或千金

A TROUBLED MIND

withered scrub
        where thick mist
                clings
forest campfires'
        fitful
            flicker

fog-banks shrouding
           countless footsteps
                on the move
Jiangsu's war-fever:
        lasting
              how much longer?

ruined villages
        enfeoffed

while barren backlands
          starve

medicine-chests
          all ransacked

        while skilled tacticians
           sit round
              killing time

ZHOU TINGZHEN (1292-1379)

憂懷　周霆震

黃落雜煙蕪林炊午有無喪氛移步滿兵氣幾時蘇
小邑疲封拜窮鄉落饋輸刦深資病減閑坐校靈樞

BALLAD OF THE NORTH WIND

beyond the wall
                north winds' mounting howl
across the wall
                blasts buffet soldiers' ears

— *swaddled in snug sable,*
                our general shifts
                                a curtain hung with jade
— *clutches his wine-cup,*
                watches snowflakes
                                flutter down

LIU JI (1311-1375)

將軍玉帳貂鼠衣手持酒杯看雪飛
城外蕭蕭北風起城上健兒吹落耳

北風行梗　劉基

EVENING MARCH: ZHANGGONG VILLAGE

rotting crops
        travellers few and far between
sequestered hamlet
    hemmed in by high hills
doorways gaping …
      empty streets …

one bird floating by
        beneath banked cloud
– icy howling of the gale …
        one crow's distant glide
           as daylight swiftly fades

our tract of time a hundred years –
      the *wutong* tree grows old
autumn winds
    across a myriad miles –
      so rice can sprout in spring

Mongol soldiers' trampling
        raises dust
   blurring the road home
     north of the Yellow River:
endless gloomy shoals of sand
        gilded by sun's last rays …

   MA GE (Yuan dynasty)

晚步張翬田間　麻革

地入荒蕪過客稀村深門巷莫山圍
悠悠獨鳥穿雲下策策寒烏掠日飛
人事百年梧葉老秋風萬裡稻花肥
兵塵河朔迷歸路惆悵平沙送夕暉

A SOLDIER'S WOMAN VENTS HER GRIEF

did he ever crave promotion or a title, my poor husband?
      the tiger tally of enlistment took him far away
and many nightmares came to haunt my bedroom

now the general's HQ sends a letter:
      our armies all are overthrown …
he's dead, my man – but here's his battledress, at least

a neighbour, his old comrade, brought it back
      I've been a courtesan my whole life long
how can I track his bones down – even find the Wuwei road?

I cut these paper banners
    to summon back his soul

here at the place where once we said farewell

    GAO QI (1336-1374)

征
婦
怨

高
啟

隻紙尋妾東身竟幾虎良
向幡骨生家沒得夜符人
當剪何不火猶將春遠不
時得由識伴存軍閨發願
送招到邊為舊軍惡當封
行魂武庭收戰覆夢番侯
處去威路歸衣信多陣印

89

Khublai's ancestral hall:
  girdled round
    by nightfall's
      afterglow

Time's green mosses
  suffocate the graven steles

Thistle Gate in Beijing's city-wall
  today we reverence
    the image left behind

why seek those ancient
    burial-grounds?

Mongol characters
  half scored
    upon a temple-pillar

paintings in the porch's gloom:
  General Boyan's armies

sad to see a withered tree
  all its blossoms gone
still spread its branches

by day
  owl's eldritch hooting

          reaches deepest night

MA ZHONGYANG (1450-1516)

瞻元世祖廟　馬中錫

世祖祠堂帶夕曛
碧苔年久暗碑文
薊門此日瞻遺像
起輦何人識故墳

棹楔半存蒙古字
陰廊尚繪伯顏軍
可憐老樹無花發
白晝鵁鳴到夜分

90

CROSSING THE BORDER

barbarians spread out to the Yellow River's banks
        men of Qin are slain – the Great Wall stays intact

shifting desert sands ... a setting sun ...
        then icy mists
                as we bed down in watch-towers
                        scattered here and there

scouts to recce the three borderlands:
        a thousand *li* we slash and burn at dusk

our generals lusting for the golden seal of office
        never giving all our dead a moment's thought

LI MENGYANG (1473-1529)

將軍拜金印白骨不曾論
哨馬三邊動燒荒千裡昏
磧沙浮落日寒霧宿疏墩
胡蔓黃河限秦亡紫塞存

出塞　李夢陽

FAREWELL COMMANDER LI: OFF TO YUNZHONG

yellow winds from the north:
     fog-bale thickens
bold Yunzhou warriors
     blow their horns

the general smooths his sword-blade –
     waits for dawn …
Hegan mountain shudders
     a waning moon slips down

horses whinny at mangers
     soldiers scoff their provender
once they wore rags
     now furs and embroidery

with loosened reins
     they scud over sands
aim shots at birds of prey

     autumn floods the plain with grasses –

barbarian chieftains run away

  LI MENGYANG (1473-1529)

送李帥之雲中　李夢陽

黃風北來雲氣惡雲州健兒夜吹角
將軍按劍坐待曙紀干山搖月半落
槽頭馬鳴士飯飽昔無完衣今綉襖
沙場緩彎行射鵰秋草滿地單于逃

ON THE BORDER: A MISCELLANEOUS POEM

daily, nightly, beaconfires
　　　　along the borderlands
urgent orders reach us:
　　　　muster your troops!
sheep and oxen now return
　　　　to our lofty stronghold
dogs and poultry
　　　　all sense our alarm
soldiers smooth swordblades,
　　　　hefting them high
our cavalry swoop
　　　　flashing like firedrakes
spearpoints press onward –
　　　　thousands collapsing
we laugh at the fallen:
　　　　they yield up their forts …
all we now live for:
　　　　to capture five chieftains
hauling them home:
　　　　parade them at Court!

　LI MENGYANG (1473-1529)

生繫五單於歸來獻天庭
鎗急萬人靡笑上受降城
壯士按劍起鞍馬若流星
羊牛入高砦雞犬皆震驚
邊烽日夜至飛符來會兵

塞上雜詩　李夢陽

MORNINGS WATERING MY HORSE:
FAREWELL MASTER CHEN, OFF TO THE FRONTIER

mornings take my horse to water
evenings take my horse to water

salty water: will he drink it? no
dried-up grasses: will he eat them? no

all those passing underneath the Wall
                    shedding bitter tears ...

beside its battlements: strewn corpses: can you tell me whose?

someone says: *'this year's forced labourers –*
their only road led far from homes and kinfolk:
not knowing how each man's nine lives
would all be spent
(not one goes back alive)

            and would they mind their bodies crumbling to dust beneath the city-walls?
            this, however – this they do regret:
            all their labour spent for other people's profit and reward

last year bandits plundered Kaifeng county:
            blood gushed beneath Black Mountain
                        where savage chieftains' arrows found their mark

across so many miles of yellow dust
            our cries shook heaven

every day they close the city gates: no one dares fight

and so this year they issue orders: "fortify our borders!"
  and navvies toil half-dead before the Wall

blanched grasses north and south of it
  louring clouds at sunset

    clanking, clashing of barbarian flails'

LI MENGYANG (1473-1529)

朝飲馬送陳子出塞　李夢陽

朝飲馬夕飲馬
水鹹草枯馬不食行人痛哭長城下城邊白骨借問誰是今年築城者
但道辭家別六親寧知九死無還身不惜身為城下土所恨功成賞別人
去年賊掠開成縣黑山血逬單于箭萬裡黃塵哭震天城門晝閉無人戰
今年下令修築邊丁夫半死長城前城南城北秋草白愁雲日暮鳴胡鞭

95

harsh keen air now:
    autumn arrives
nomads on horseback
    harass our border towns
the emperor's orders
    flash with meteoric speed –
fresh conscripts levied
    at dead of night
and so we push forward:
    strict fish-scale formation
        according to plan
the emperor's guards
    seize their chance – *charge!*
white spear-blades cross:
    as they cross, clashing
each bow curving back:
    moons at the full
their swift- flying barbs
    sing loud before falling
blood gushes out
    reddens the grasses …
deep pits crammed
    brimful of corpses –
soldiers wash themselves
    in Longshui's waters
war-spoils all yielded
    at Chengming Gate
horror, shock and awe:
    our emperor's wisdom
numbing the nomads
    scattered asunder
deep understanding
    informs the whole plan
for this he appointed
    a single great scholar
his strategy smashed them
    those skirmishing bandits

    GU LIN (1476-1545)

戰城南　顧璘

嚴秋朔氣至敵騎寇邊城軍符星流急中夜起徵兵
魚麗按圖列龍韜應機呈前軍白刃交格鬥聲鏦錚
控弦若滿月飛鏑競先鳴流血原草赤填尸坑谷平
洗兵下隴水獻捷奏承明天威赫神武戎狄震且驚
孰知折衝略乃由一書生伐謀貴廟算匪在多戰爭

FOLLOWING THE ARMY

when young you lust for glory
      your only topics: warriors and swordplay
with high hopes you enlist
      wrongly dreaming of a marquisate

one fine morning your small squad falls in
      not knowing how much toil and trouble lies in store

      in the southwest scour those distant tribes!
      in the northeast take barbarians captive!
the Martial Emperor has a mighty plan
    he wants to blaze new trails
      and open up new territories ...

you follow orders,
      gallop gallant steeds as fierce as you
the generals who command you
      like those of ancient times
(but these same generals take the credit for your feats)

      troops are told to spread beyond the border
      push far east beyond the mountain passes
through barren lands your war machine will clank
that bleak back-country: you'll lay it all to waste

      war's what court-plotters covet most
         carve right through all frontiers whether north or south
equipment's needed urgently – with meteoric speed –
      (but troops pour out for years and years and years)

warships set off into turbid waters
      horses plunge across Tibetan snows
and yet you've still not covered half those rivers, mountains

      you're now so worn out that your hair's quite thin

consumed by frostbite, soldiers' fingers drop off
their flesh shrivels roasted by hot winds
when sick for home their tears are all dried up
their hearts are broken when they gaze afar
anger and sorrow: poured-out tears and sweat
hesitant on cliff-edges, icy and vertiginous
far far away through alien lands
hazardous pathways leaning to one side

who would enter the cave of a tiger?
who can subdue the tribes of Guiming?

secret envoys sent
to set the Kunming savage tribes at odds
armies cut off, bogged down in Kashgar ...

but say the army has some luck –
the faces of those pen-pushers lose colour

now Fate has murder in her heart:
she foments heroes' fury
the tips of arrows loosed in flight
sound like rushing winds
blood saturates the garments
of all those they impale

five kingdoms always roused to war
circling round and round to certain ruin

'advance' banners lead you on
for many thousand miles
till you return with all three armies
playing victory tunes

that day throughout the borderlands
       war has ceased at last …
"when all the birds are killed,
       the bow is cast aside" …

walk a straight path,
       the penpushers detest you
merit high advancement,
       and your colleagues just feel envy
tick all the boxes for reward,
       you're sure to be excluded:
              letters will defame you, stitch you up
the white-haired soldier who returns:
       a convict standing in the dock condemned!
          strain every sinew for your lord,
              can he even tell the difference
                 between the true and the duplicitous?
the stout heart bright as any sun
       the flashing sword of valour,
          heroes mounting to the clouds

       and all of it in vain, in vain

who can determine
       the ways of this world?
who hopes to fathom
       the dictates of destiny?

in that Hall of Fame, the 'Unicorn Pavilion',
       there's one portrait
          you'll surely never see:

       our greatest border general, Li Guang!

Xue Hui (1489-1541)

從軍行　薛蕙

少小慕功名擊劍復談兵誤信封侯事甘作從軍行
一朝備行伍幾處罹辛苦西南通遠夷東北攘驕虜
武帝雄材略土宇新開拓銜命馳嚴馬登壇延衛霍諸將竟邀功
歲歲出臨戎勒兵盈塞外發卒遍關東
騷屑干戈動蕭條田野空廟謀貪戰伐邊隙開胡粵軍興急星火兵連淹歲月戈船下屬水策馬逾蔥雪
山川行未半容鬢凋換寒冰手指墮炎風肌肉爛思鄉已淚盡腸斷怫郁魚泣津凌兢猿眩岸
悠悠歷絕國險道何傾側虎穴詎可入鬼方寧易克間使閉昆明單兵陷疏勒全軍有天幸從吏無人色
天時變殺機壯士奮兵威飛矢風鳴鏑推兵血濺衣長驅五王國大破九重圍萬裡懸旌出三軍赭衣從吏議
邊垂日無事鳥盡良弓棄行直責臣憎功高同列忌賞格多排沮謗書仍負累白頭還士伍奏凱歸
輸力奉明君忠邪不見分丹心徒貫日劍氣枉凌雲人事竟莫測天命諒難聞可憐麟閣上不畫李將軍

ON THE BORDER: TWO POEMS

warfare without end: dry bones …
     clear autumn skies – the steppe goes on and on
soaring eagles circle: barren lands …
     horses whinny – make the deep woods shudder
The Son of Heaven pacified the tribes
     ennobled doughty warriors for their courage
our common world has its own natural limits
     all this crossing borders to invade – what for?

frontier fortress in the fall:
     a hard frost fills the air
daily patrols, reporting back,
     ride through the yamen's gate
bad news from the battle-front
     has blanched the general's hair
no one knows how many soldiers lost …
     battered armour, tattered rags …

XIE ZHEN (1495-1575)

塞上曲　謝榛

百戰多枯骨秋高白草深飛雕盤大漠嘶馬振長林
柔遠君王德封侯壯士心華夷自有限邊徼莫相侵

101

LEAVING THE BORDER

the general leaves in splendour

     but the borderlands he's quelled
         remain unlovely …

         a barren darkness
           smothered by deep snows
       or else beset
          by yellow dust-tornadoes

at dawn beside the river –
     barbarian tents
as night descends,
     those tribal chiefs carouse

        their sons go dancing,
          flapping narrow sleeves
        their matchless sable coats
          smelling of sweet musk …

   XU WEI (1521-1593)

出塞　徐渭

漢將去堂堂
邊塵靖不揚
雪沈荒漠暗
沙攬塞風黃

虜帳朝依水
胡酋夜進觴
舞兒回袖窄
無奈紫貂香

102

DESOLATION ON THE BATTLEFIELD

swarming round
      the general's feathered banner
scaly armour ripples, glitters

drive on through barbarian lands
        dusk thickening around you

a single tragedy, this battlefield –
      but numberless the tears shed by
these bold souls
      none of whom return
          nameless in the shadowlands below

bleached bones scattered and heaped up
      familiar to the moon
        revisiting
          these frontier passes

rock-piles mark each grave
      raked by blasts of northern wind

darkling clouds
      sandstorms, snowstorms flying overhead
hurtling gales –

      follow that bugle-call

          come to certain grief

   XUE LUNDAO (?1531-?1600)

朔風日日吹雲迷驚沙帶雪飛風催人隨戰角悲

英魄歸未歸黃泉誰是誰森森白骨塞月常常會塚塚磧堆

擁旌庵鱗鱗隊隊度胡天昏昏昧昧戰場一吊多少征人淚

北中呂・山坡羊　吊戰場　薛論道

103

still not put down, those northern tribes?
              brave men inly rage

a waste of time,
         me worrying
                dawn to dusk:

           those savage courts will never swim in blood …

– but to let the dust fly round
              their rank disorder!

                what an insult to the nation!

O once-mighty China:
         where are your heroes now?

our miserable white-polled elders
                  wring their hands

      while glib tongues flatter:

           those pen-pushers'
              billowing black gowns!

    XUE LUNDAO (?1531-?1600)

【仙呂・桂枝香】宿將自悲　薛論道

匈奴未滅壯懷激烈空勞宵旰憂賢哪見虜庭喋血任胡塵亂飛侮
辱郊社堂堂中國誰是豪傑蕭蕭白發長扼腕滾滾青衫弄巧舌

ON THE BORDER

beside the waters of the Wuding River
>> *keening winter sounds*
>>>> *whip above white sands*
last month's cities yielded to the foe:
>> *twilight veils*
>>>> *the moaning of a flute*

atop the general's tent: a star portending war
>> *– over the Altai mountains*
>>>> *a V-shaped skein of geese*
… and once the campaign's over,
>> *how many heroes*
>>>> *ever make it home?*

    Ao Ying (Ming dynasty)

塞上曲　敖英

無定河邊水寒聲走白沙受降城上月暮色隱悲笳
玉帳旌頭落金微雁陣斜幾時征戰息壯士盡還家

FIGHTING SOUTH OF THE WALL

South of the Wall we fight,
By the battlements south of the Wall.
North of the wall black clouds lour;
Infantry lurking over to the east,
       waiting for the chance of an ambush
Cavalry scatter over to the west
       harry our flanks without mercy.
Brown dust rising around us –
The sun growing darker and darker –
       the whole sky a haze.
Clamour of gongs and drums:
Shrieks and yells of the dying.
Barbarian horsemen retreating,
Flying back swift as a storm.
The stark trees sickly as weeds,
The grass bleached white and dry.

Who's that crying in the ruck?
A father bears his son's limp corpse.
Wives come seeking their husbands –
Pikes and breastplates in piles,
Skulls smeared red with blood.
Each family summons a soul,
Each company mourns its men.

Go tell our General
If he doesn't know this already.
When living we fought on the frontier
Why should we care
       if they bury us here on the steppes?
The rations in the pot
Grew cold at noon …
Too bad! We sprang to arms,
       and then we parted for ever.
Our meals were left unfinished …

The wind howls over the dunes
and our souls are running with the wind.

They should go look at the General
Sitting up there in the fort
under the banner of gold
grasping his ivory baton.
While he lives they'll grant him high titles.
When he dies and goes to his ancestors,
No shortage of food at *his* grave.

WANG SHIZHEN (1526-1590)

戰城南　王世貞

戰城南城南壁黑雲壓我城北伏兵搗我東游騎抄我西
使我不得休息
黃塵合匝日為青天模糊鉦鼓發亂謹呼胡騎斂飆迅驅
樹若薺草為枯啼者何父收子妻問夫戈甲委積血淹頭
顧家家招魂入隊隊自哀呼
告主將主將若不知生為邊陲士野葬復何悲釜中食午
未炊惜其倉皇遂長訣焉得一飽為野風騷屑魂依之曷
不睹主將高牙大纛坐城中生當封徹侯死當廟食無窮

107

ON THE BORDER

Xiongnu stronghold sacked:
        snow there's turned to slush
                under Tassel Mountain
                        sparrows chirrup spring
March chock-full now
        of orioles and fresh flowers –
                all our slain head south
                        to haunt their widows' dreams

say someone follows rank:
        meets with defeat, misfortune –
                his border-spirit rises in the reeds
                        nightly with the wildgeese ...
Majesty, magnanimous and merciful,
        if you'd not sent so many
                        off to slaughter
        maybe fewer living men
                would enter Jade Gate Pass
                      never to return

Gu Yanwu (1613-1682)

塞下曲二首　顧炎武

信城邊雪化塵紀乾山下雀呼春即今三月鶯花滿長作江南夢裡人

趙

一從都尉生降去夜夜魂隨塞雁蘆陞下寬仁多不殺可能生入玉門無

108

autumn mountains upon autumn mountains …
     autumn rains: thunder rumbles through a mountain range
fighting at the river-mouth, just one day past
     today more fighting on the mountainside
first the right flank's gone, I hear
     now those resisting on the left have been destroyed
earth covers all our banners …
     scaling ladders, battle rams:
        how they dance before the south gate of our city!
         think back to ancient Changping:
            in just one morning genocidal slaughter
         corpses of the vanquished everywhere
          heaped up ever higher, mound on mound
bound northward these three hundred barges –
     each barge laden with our rouge-cheeked girls
        many camels cluster on our quays:
        skreaking foreign fifes pierce Swallow Pass …
        once men of Yan and men of Ying
         refused to serve the Qin:
south of the capital such warriors still exist …

                    GU YANWU (1613-1682)

秋山　顧炎武

秋山復秋山殷
昨日戰江口今日戰山邊
已聞右甄潰復見左拒殘
旌旗埋地中梯衝舞城端
一朝長平敗伏尸遍岡巒
北去三百舸舸舸好紅顏
吳口擁橐駝鳴笳入燕關
昔時鄗郚人猶在城南間

109

QIANTANG BEACH-HEAD LAMENTATION

sleek and lush those riverside grasses
      lashing, drumming of torrential rain

cold the spears of all those slain in battle
      yet their hatred burns afresh

sandbank firefly glitter
      scribbles on the moon's reflection

an autumn night in darkened chambers
      wraiths that moan and gibber

on a far peak, struck for the final time
      the gong falls silent and all's still

geese honk winging over
      the stark abandoned village

deep hush now: the baffled spirits
      slide after boats of the vanquished

intense grief-harrowed "droop-headed millet"
      mourning the bows unstrung

bankside wildflower roots
      with just rank blood to drink

dawn wayfarers will groan
      as jet-black demons arise

high hopes have had to follow
      cold mists that move by moonlight

what hope for a fragrant name after death
      when paper banners summon hungry ghosts?

while from her boudoir window
      the widow's lonely lamp …

don't listen to the sound of water
      don't wait up for the evening tide …

WANG DUANSHU (1621-1706?)

吊錢塘戰場　王端淑

萋萋岸草雨瀟瀟戰死寒戈恨未銷沙際螢光沉月影陰房鬼淚泣秋宵
敲殘遠岫鍾初寂喉徹荒村雁已嘹默默驚魂隨敗楫離離故黍悼空弨
野花根畔惟羶血過客朝吟帶墨妖雄志今隨烟月冷芳名何處紙旛招
深閨亦有孤燈婦莫聽江聲待晚潮

111

TUNE: 'A LOVE THAT NEVER ENDS'

one uphill journey
one upriver journey

– push your body on towards Yu Pass

      midnight: lampglow
            through a thousand tents

windblast: watchman's drum
snowblast: watchman's drum

to tear the heart
      that dreams of home

          to tear its dreams

home: where such sounds
         are never heard at all

  NALAN XINGDE (1655-1685)

長相思　納蘭成德

山一程
水一程
身向榆關那畔行
夜深千帳鐙

風一更
雪一更
聒碎鄉心夢不成
故園無此聲

TUNE: 'BODDHISATTVA BARBARIAN'

midwinter:
        wild winds pummel the ground

unbuckling your saddle –

crows that bicker ...
           darkening skies

     – river flows by icebound

          your sore heart swells and widens

emptiness, barrenness,
    far as the eye can see –

drums and trumpets
          from high city walls

you reach Chang'an tomorrow

          but your troubles travel on

          NALAN XINGDE (1655-1685)

菩薩蠻　納蘭成德

驚飆掠地冬將半解鞍正值昏鴉亂
合大河流茫茫一片愁燒痕空極望冰
角高城上明日近長安客心愁未闌
鼓

113

CROSSING THE BORDER

lean into this sheer slope
      look down towards the sea
            that ancient frontier sector …

beneath these flapping banners' shade
      see those barrack buildings yonder

behind my horse peach-blossom
      before it, driving snow

dropping down from the pass –
      hard not to cast
            one last backward glance

XU LAN (17th-18th centuries)

出關　徐蘭

憑山俯海古邊州旆影翻飛見戍樓
馬後桃花馬前雪出關爭得不回頭

p. 45 Yɪɴɢᴢʜᴏᴜ Sᴏɴɢ

Other versions of the first line provide different fifth characters: variously, instead of 滿 'fill', these read in English as 厭 'loathe', 歇 rest' and 愛 'love'. If I'd chosen the last of these, which also works well, my first line would read: 'Yingzhou's young bucks love the open prairies.'

p. 49 – Fɪᴠᴇ Fʀᴏɴᴛɪᴇʀ Sᴏɴɢs

敞: one source reads "蔽".

p 53 Aʀʀᴏᴡʜᴇᴀᴅ

1. The full title tells us that the arrowhead was found by the poet on the ancient battlefield of Changping (where, a thousand years earlier, some 400,000 Zhao warriors had allegedly been buried alive after surrendering to the forces of Qin – the same forces who, not many decades afterwards, would unify China for the first time at the cost of a huge amount of bloodshed).

2. These two kinds of spirit, the earth-bound hún (to the right) and the heavenly pò (to the left), cannot separate because proper funeral rites had been lacking: they're trapped on the battlefield. Li He will try and appease them.

3. The bamboo tray seems disappointingly anti-climactic until we realize that it would be used to offer up a sacrifice for the dead warriors' souls.

N.B. Careful readers will have noticed how skilfully each image seems to lead to the next: for instance, the 'red clay' (dān shuǐ shā) preceding the 'old blood' (gǔ xuè), and the later red of sunset; the 'steeds' (mǎ) anticipating the 'courier station' (yì); the sinister 'starved shades keening' (pò tí jī shòu) followed immediately by the 'gnat-swarms' (chóng qī) and 'geese' (yàn bìng – literally geese who are either 'distressed' or 'sick'). Li He is known in China as guǐcái or 'demon-gifted', and the creepy, morbid, 'Gothic' atmosphere of this poem is entirely typical of much of his work. Analogies with our own fin-de-siècle poètes maudits and Décadents are often made by modern commentators, and with good reason.

p. 62 Sᴇᴛᴛɪɴɢ ᴏᴜᴛ ᴇᴀʀʟʏ ʙᴇɴᴇᴀᴛʜ ᴀ Mᴏᴜɴᴛᴀɪɴ Pᴀss

愛 [?] I've taken the liberty of assuming that line 2 is corrupt: a bold thing for a translator to do. I strongly suspect that 雞 jī is a mistake: chickens on a mountain? But 潗 jí (the trickling sound of a stream as it tumbles over rocks) makes much better sense in this context. There's another onomatopoeic term in the first half of this line, and a second one would balance it. The manuscripts of Tang poems had been copied and re-copied, sometimes over many centuries, before first appearing in print. Textual errors must have proliferated, as in all such manuscript transmissions. Shakespeare scholars have made much more daring suggestions about the texts of many Shakespeare plays – and the First Folio was printed a mere seven years after his death.

p. 73 June 12th, 1233 – Crossing North: Three Verses

A small confession relating to 過去旌車似水流 My first version of this line (the one previously printed in a little magazine) read as follows: 'banners, chariots pouring past, a flood …' Only later did I become aware that the phrase 旌車 zhān chē in line 2, which does literally translate as "banners and chariots", and would have meant this in any earlier dynasty, had, nevertheless, during the Yuan dynasty, a much narrower and more specialised meaning: it meant the "felt-covered wagons" used then (and still used) by the Mongols. For a long time, I was so pleased with my original version, and particularly with this line as it then stood, that I left the mistake in. To correct it would (or so I rather desperately told myself) have ruined the rhythm. In fact I just thought that the image of 'banners and chariots' was more Romantic (however anachronistic). Willis Barnstone, a fine American translator, recently wrote that "A translator's reward for a mistake must be capital punishment" and fiercely added that there is no "freedom to make errors". In which case I was for a while on Death Row. But I then changed my mind – and I think that now the problem has been solved, albeit at the cost of a little extra (felt) padding.

ABOUT THE POETS

The Shijing ('Classic of Poetry'), from which the first two anonymous poems are taken, is traditionally believed to have been compiled by Confucius. The poems it contains are certainly very ancient, many of them probably more or less contemporaneous with Homer (*c.* 800 BCE). All subsequent Chinese classical poetry stems from this one book.

WANG CAN (177-217) is considered to have been the most outstanding of what were known as the Seven Masters of the Jian'an Era (which covered the end of the Han dynasty and the start of the Six Dynasties). The so-called three 'Seven Sorrows', two of which are included, are among his most famous extant compositions. He threw in his lot with the great general Cao Cao (of 'Three Kingdoms' fame), and was greatly respected by that formidable warlord.

RUAN JI (210-263) is the most celebrated member of that somewhat dissolute group of scholars and poets known as 'The Seven Sages of the Bamboo Grove', and was by far the greatest poet of his era.

BAO ZHAO (*c.* 414-466) was a fifth-century poet who wrote particularly fine 'border poems' in the traditional 樂府 yuèfǔ ('ballad') genre, two of which are included here. Because of his marginal involvement in a rebellion, he was executed in 466.

CHEN SHUBAO (553-604) was the last emperor of the short-lived minor dynasty (557-589) known as the Chen (after his family name). He presided over a court devoted to the arts, and was himself an accomplished minor poet.

LU ZHAOLIN (*c.* 635-689), is another member of one of those quaintly named literary groups of which the Chinese are so fond, in this case 'The Four Paragons of the Early Tang'. Although later dismissed by the great Du Fu as 'not a serious' poet, he was in fact a writer of singular strength and originality. He suffered terribly in his last years from what may have been a crippling form of rheumatoid arthritis. In the end, the pain grew too great for him to bear, and he drowned himself.

Little is known about LIU XIYI 劉希夷 (*c.* 651-*c.* 680) today, though he was highly rated in his own time. Not much of his work survives. He is not to be confused with the homophonous somewhat later and

117

much greater Liu Xiyi 劉禹錫 (772-842). One account of the earlier poet's death states that it occurred as the result of a single, allegedly slanderous, couplet he had written. If true, this would arguably have been taking the literary critic's rôle in life a little too seriously.

WANG CHANGLING (c. 690-c. 756) was an important poet and literary critic, who specialised in 'border poetry'. He was killed during the terrible An Lushan rebellion (755-763). Many of the significant works by him that we know about were lost during the later part of the Tang dynasty.

LI QI (690-751) was a close acquaintance of both Wang Wei and Wang Changling. He was a bit of an eccentric, with eremitic tendencies and a love of alchemy. His work is said to have been strongly influenced by Li Bai (see below).

WANG WEI (?691-761), along with Li Bai and Du Fu, was one of the three titans of High Tang poetry. The stillness, clarity and deep sense of Buddhist negation that one finds, especially in his quatrains but also in much of his other poetry, have endeared him to Chinese and Western readers alike.

GAO SHI (704-765) was yet another member of that circle of High Tang poets mentioned above. Unlike any of the others, he had a distinguished military and political career. He and his contemporary, Cen Shen (not represented in this anthology), have always been coupled together in terms of their fondness for 'border-style' poetry.

WANG HAN (fl. 720) was a somewhat debauched figure, only fourteen of whose poems now survive, despite the high reputation he enjoyed in his own day. The seven-word lines of the quatrain translated here comprise his most famous poem.

CUI HAO (704-754). Here we encounter yet another aristocratic poet who believed in living life to the full while challenging social conventions; though his poetry was much less adventurous. He is remembered for one superb poem ('Yellow Crane Tower') which not long afterwards inspired the much greater Li Bai to try and emulate it, though (as Li himself admitted) without success. The poem included here is not so well known, though it is another fine example of 'border' poetry.

DU FU (712-770) and LI BAI (701-762) are often thought of as the two front-runners for the title of 'China's Greatest Poet'. Du's technical mastery and the range and depth of his work set him apart from all of his contemporaries. The An Lushan rebellion made him a refugee and separated him from his family. He wrote powerfully about the experience of fleeing through a country torn apart by conflict.

Lu Lun (748-799?) was a widely travelled poet, whose employment on the staff of the Military Commissioner of Hezhong took him directly into the regions he describes in his lively frontier verses.

Bao Junhui (*fl.* 798), one of the Tang dynasty's relatively small band of female poets, was considered to be a scholar of distinction as well as a talented versifier, and in both capacities she attracted the emperor Dezong's attention.

Zu Yong (*fl.* 8th century). In his childhood he had been a friend of Wang Wei; while still quite a young man, he retired from court, and the majority of his poems adopt pastoral themes. The poem by which he is represented here is in many respects atypical.

Li He (790-816) was one of a group of highly talented late Tang poets whose abstruse and ornately stylized verses often deliberately courted obscurity. He himself was drawn towards the uncanny and the macabre, which helps to explain the considerable attraction his poetry holds for many Western readers, and the glamour that dazzled many later Chinese poets.

Wen Tingyun (801?-866) is a poet whose skimpy biography contains much that is merely anecdotal and about whom, in reality, little is known for certain (he may or may not have earned his later reputation as a rake). What is definite is that he excelled in two genres: the 樂府 yuèfǔ or 'ballad', and, more influentially, the 詞 cí or 'lyric', which he helped to pioneer.

Wei Zhuang (836-910) is best known for the splendid long narrative poem entitled 'Lament by a Lady from Qin', lost for over a millennium, and discovered in the Dunhuang caves at the start of the twentieth century. The much shorter sardonic poem translated here is a tersely worded comment on the folly of all war.

Ma Dai (*fl.* 9th century) was moved around from one minor administrative post to another, suffering the usual vicissitudes of imperial favour, before ending his career as Court Academician in the prestigious 'Taixue' or National University. Little else is known about him.

119

ZHANG QIAO (Tang Dynasty) lived through the increasingly turbulent final decades of the Tang dynasty. The Huang Chao rebellion ended his hopes of a career in the imperial administration, and from then on he lived in retirement.

LIN KUAN (Tang Dynasty) is shrouded in obscurity and only a few of his poems survive. Both of those included in this anthology suggest personal experience of life in the borderlands.

LIU KAI (947-1000) was, on the one hand, an accomplished scholar and poet and, on the other, a savagely cruel military commander. Such a combination of qualities is by no means unique in Chinese history.

ZHAO BINGWEN (1159-1232) was a distinguished neo-Confucian philosopher as well as one of the leading poets serving under the Jin (Jurchen) dynasty. He was praised by Yuan Haowen (see below), who wrote his biography.

LIU KEZHUANG (1187-1269) was "the most prolific writer of the thirteenth century", according to the *Indiana Companion to Traditional Chinese Literature*. But there was quality in abundance to complement the sheer quantity of his output. He was an important literary critic as well as one of the leading scholars and poets of the Southern Song.

YELÜ CHUCAI (1190-1244) is a most attractive figure in Chinese history. His tall stature, long beard and sonorous voice made him a memorable figure both among his contemporaries and subsequent generations. He persuaded both Genghis and Ögedei Khan that taxing the Han Chinese was much more profitable than slaughtering them in droves; in this way he saved countless lives. He was descended from a long line of Khitan aristocrats. He accompanied Genghis Khan during a long expedition to the remote West in 1218, and wrote an account of it that can still be read with profit and enjoyment today.

YUAN HAOWEN (1190-1257) is a major figure in Chinese literature, not just as a poet, but also as a historian. It is worth noting that the great Japanese scholar Yoshikawa Kōjirō has boldly maintained that he "may well be the foremost Chinese poet from Du Fu to the present". He lived through the calamitous fall of the Jin, the dynasty which he had always served faithfully, and his *sangluan* poetry of witness is unparalleled in its eloquence and compassion. He has hitherto been poorly served by English translators.

Duan Keji (1196-1254) and his brother Duan Chengji, known to their contemporaries as the 'Two Marvels', were the most famous of a group of followers of Yuan Haowen. Like him they lived through a time of genocidal carnage and, wisely one feels, lived lives of retirement from public affairs (keeping one's head down was probably the best way not to lose it to the flash of a Mongol sword).

Wang Zhong (*fl.* 13th century). That he lived towards the very end of the Southern Song, and that his courtesy name was 'Jiweng' is all the information that can currently be gleaned about him.

Gong Kai (1222-1307) was an official under the Southern Song. Intensely loyal to this regime long after it had fallen to the Mongols, he refused to serve under the Yuan, and whereas others in the same predicament turned to writing plays, he took up painting as a means of keeping body and soul together. This poem accompanied his most famous picture, in which the horse is a symbol both of the defeated dynasty and of its now impoverished intelligentsia.

Hao Jing (1233-1275) was a Neo-Confucian scholar and an advisor to Khubilai Khan. On that ruler's behalf, he attempted to effect some kind of reconciliation between the Southern Song and the ascendant Mongols. and was, in other words, a peacemaker. Needless to say, his appeals fell on deaf ears, and he was imprisoned by the Song for a decade and a half.

Song Wu (1260-*c*. 1340), then just a humble clerk in the army, was one of the few survivors of the disastrous armada sent by Khubilai Khan against Japan. His style was heavily influenced by late Tang verse, in particular that of Li He.

Zhang Yanghao (1269-1329) wrote one of the most famous extant 怀古 huáigǔ poems, called 'Lamenting the Past at Tong Pass', of which several English translations exist. The verses he wrote towards the end of his life, when he was a government official in Guanzhong at a time of drought and famine, focus memorably on the sufferings of the common people.

Zhou Tingzhen (1292-1379) is particularly well-known for his 喪亂 sāngluàn poems about the turbulent era through which he lived.

121

Liu Ji (1311-1375) was not just a poet, but also a philosopher and a statesman, who wrote about military strategy while assisting the founder of the Ming dynasty to oust the Mongols from China.

Ma Ge (Yuan Dynasty), another friend of Yuan Haowen, was Assistant Minister in the Ministry of War under the Jin. Like his much more famous friend, he suffered under the Mongol invasions, and wrote well about the privations he endured.

Gao Qi (1336-1374) is widely believed to be one of the very greatest Ming dynasty poets. The notoriously cruel Hongwu emperor had him sliced into eight parts for his alleged involvement in a rebellion.

Ma Zhongyang (1450-1516) was both an imperial Censor and an Assistant Minister in the Ministry of War. But to be an official under the Ming could be dangerous, especially if you fell foul of the eunuchs, who wielded great influence at court. Ma Zhongyang died in prison.

Wang Pan (c. 1470-1530) was a highly cultivated painter and musician, whose one book of poems enjoyed a high reputation among his contemporaries.

Li Mengyang (1473-1529) was a polymath: cosmologist, historian, philosopher and leader of the 'Archaist' or 'Revivalist' movement in the arts, which favoured injecting more genuine emotion and simplicity into poetry by seeking inspiration from High Tang poets such as Du Fu. He was the foremost member of the influential group known as the 'Seven Earlier Masters'.

Gu Lin (1476-1545), who hailed from the 'Chinese Venice', Suzhou, was one of the 'Three Masters from Jinling'. He held various high offices, before enjoying a retirement graced by all the arts.

Xue Hui (1489-1541) passed the all-important jìnshì (進士) exam in 1514, and worked in the Ministry of Justice. Like many Chinese scholars, he was of a tolerant, syncretist disposition and leaned equally towards both Buddhism and Daoism.

Xie Zhen (1495-1575) was one of the 'Seven Later Masters [of the Ming]'. Although what is called a 'commoner poet' (that is, not from a privileged aristocratic background), he achieved considerable fame and popularity for his verses while still in his teens. Later on, he wrote works of literary criticism and espoused influential views on the theory of poetry.

Xu Wei (1521-1593) was a leading dramatist as well as a distinguished essayist, calligrapher and painter. When young, he had been an influential aide to Hi Zongxian, who commanded the armies responsible for defending the south of China. He is also remembered for having murdered his wife, a crime for which he spent a mere seven years in prison, thanks to the intervention of a powerful friend. Strangely, in view of this dubious record on the marital front, the female heroines of his dramas are all feisty and memorable characters, very much the superiors to their male counterparts.

Xue Lundao (?1531-1600) was a soldier for three decades, and rose to the rank of general. He was famous for his mastery of the 散曲 sǎnqǔ genre (a form of lyric poem). One charmingly entitled prose work of his is the 林石逸興 línshí yìxìng 'Taking Pleasure at One's Ease Among Rocks and Groves'. Over a thousand of his poems survive.

Ao Ying (Ming Dynasty) passed his jìnshì (進士) examination in 1522. He was a government official first in Nanjing, and then in Suzhou. He is principally remembered for the prose work entitled Dōnggǔ zhuìyán 東谷贅言 ('Superfluous Words from the Eastern Valley').

Wang Shizhen (1526-1590) was "the dominant figure in Chinese literature during much of the late sixteenth century", according to Daniel Bryant (*The Indiana Companion of Traditional Chinese Literature*). His output alone was on a staggering scale, but equally impressive was the depth and range of his best work.

Gu Yanwu (1613-1682) wrote on a wide range of subjects, among them philosophy, philology, epigraphy, phonetics, history, geography and economics (one wonders how he ever found time for his poetry). He was a Ming Loyalist who refused to serve under the Qing, although, unlike many of his friends (most of whom died for their principles), he did not actively oppose the new regime, but merely retired from public life to pursue a life of study and reflection.

Wang Duanshu (1621-1706) was a well-known Ming Loyalist woman writer, respected for her scholarship and literary accomplishments. She compiled one of the most important seventeenth-century collections of women's poetry.

NALAN XINGDE (1655-1685) was the son of a Manchu Grand Secretary, who mastered the art of the Chinese lyric poem (the 詞 cí) to such an extent by the time of his early death that, in the opinion of the great twentieth-century poet and scholar Wang Guowei, he had become the finest lyric poet since the Northern Song – praise indeed, and richly merited.

XU LAN (17th-18th centuries) was another admirer of the Late Tang poet Li He. He wrote a number of descriptive frontier poems while on an expedition to Outer Mongolia, and the strangeness both of what he saw there and of the language he used in these fine poems excited the admiration of his contemporaries.

ABOUT THE TRANSLATOR

KEVIN MAYNARD was awarded a First Class Honours BA degree at Exeter University and went on to do research into the History of Ideas at the Warburg Institute. Subsequently he became an English teacher and worked in both maintained and independent schools in London and Hertfordshire for over three decades. He came to Chinese literature quite serendipitously in his late forties, and studied Mandarin on a part-time basis at the School of Oriental and African Studies for five years. He has had poems and translations published in a range of magazines, and in 2017 one of the poems included in this anthology ('Building Walls') was 'Commended' in the Stephen Spender Prize Competition.

After spending over three decades in St Albans, Hertfordshire, he now lives on the South Coast in West Sussex.